CELESTIAL

a colorable zodiac journal

Gabriel Picolo

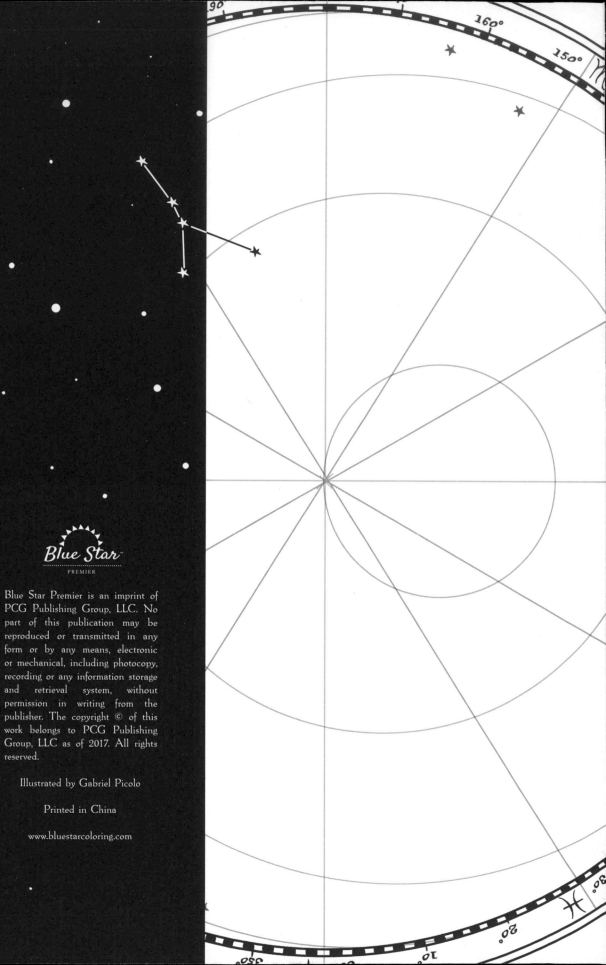

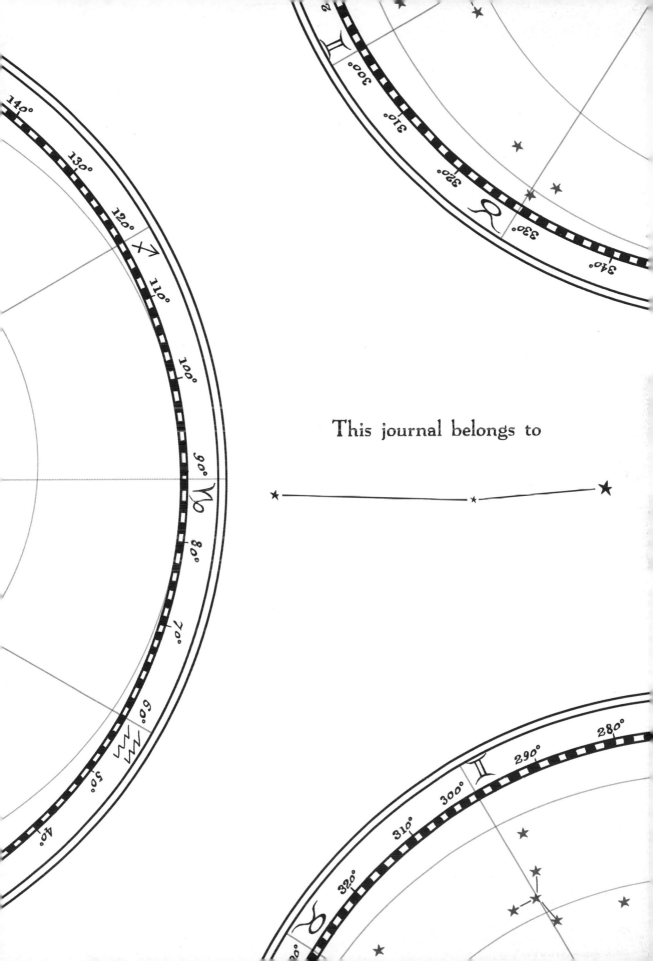

This journal belongs to

This book is intended to help you find your center and to structure your daily routines around your own personality traits. By coloring for a few minutes each day, you may find yourself in more tranquil states. This journal is intended to be malleable and can be used to write down your deepest feelings or merely keep track of your grocery lists. But regardless of how you decide to use Celestial, using it regularly can help you become more mindful and more open to the possibilities that this universe has in store for you.

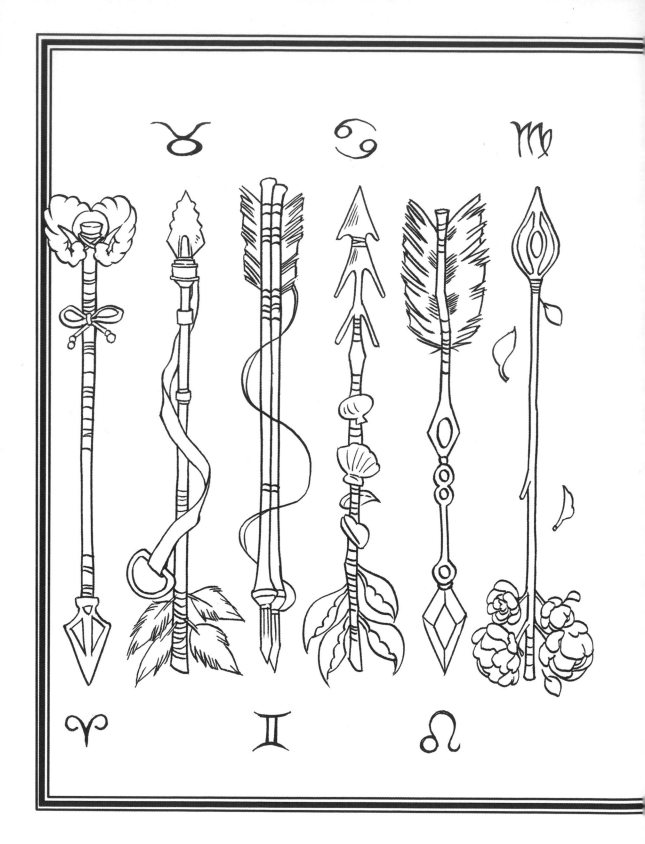

These are your guiding arrows.

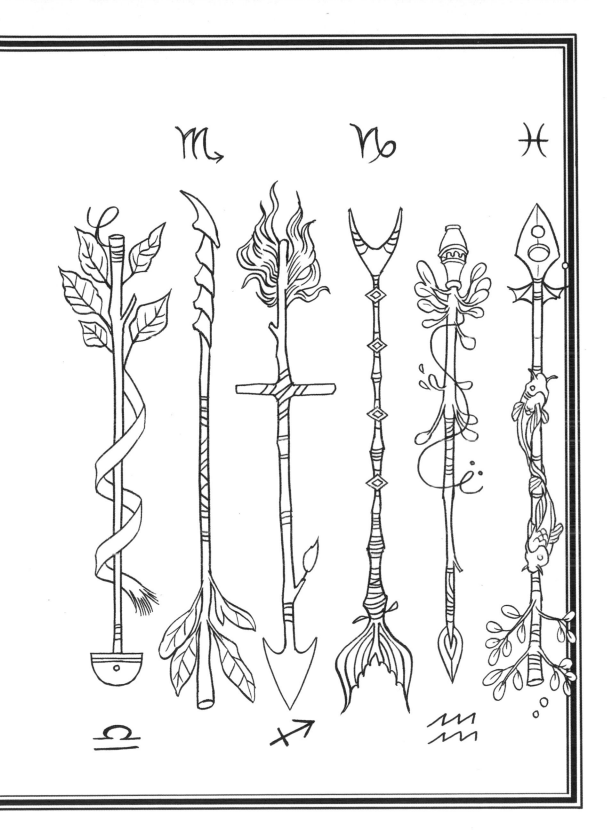

At the end of each month, color one in a color scheme that reflects that period of time. You guide the arrows as much as they guide you.

Aries were the vanguard; they invented the custom arrows. The purpose of the horns was to stake their claim on the target or territory.

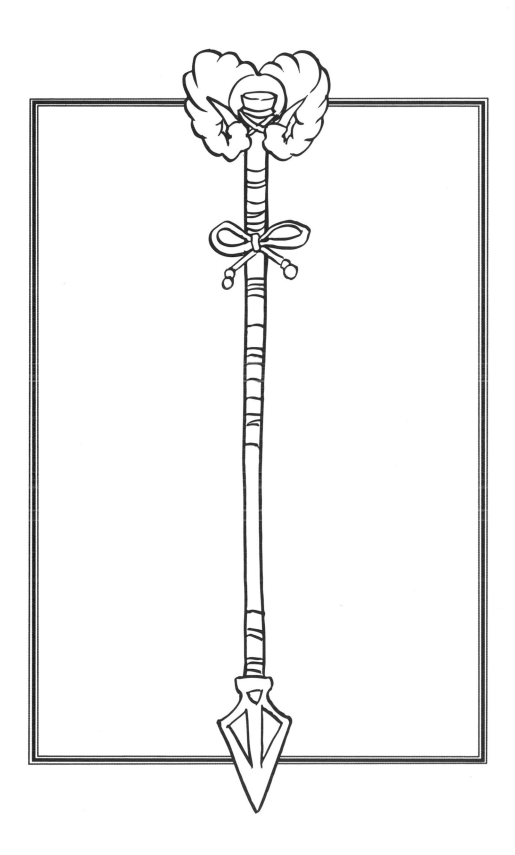

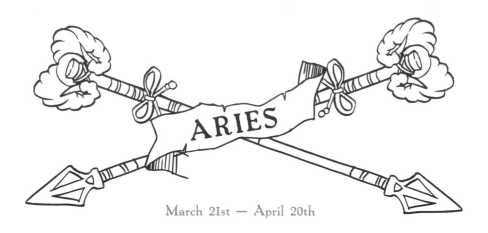

ARIES

March 21st — April 20th

To strong and courageous beginnings;
an enthusiastic start to a fresh journey.

_____
_____
_____
_____
_____
_____
_____
_____
_____
_____
_____
_____
_____
_____
_____
_____
_____
_____
_____
_____
_____
_____
_____
_____

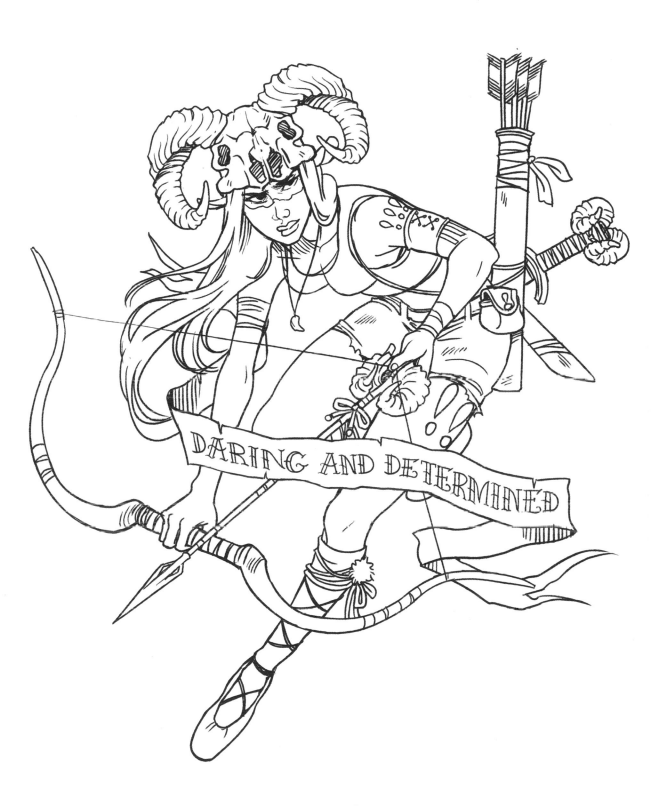

Taurus arrows are tied together with a lace that has a bull's nose ring at its end. Taurus are stubborn and don't ever give up so their arrow can be used as a spear if the fight demands it.

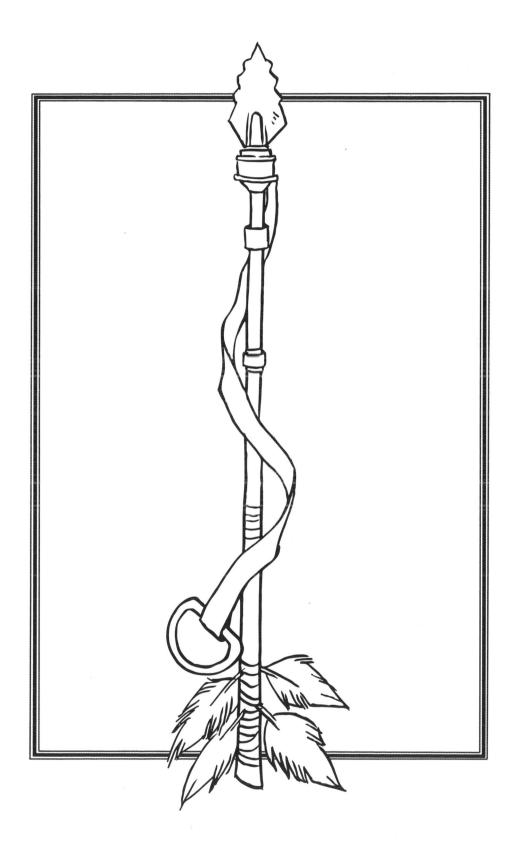

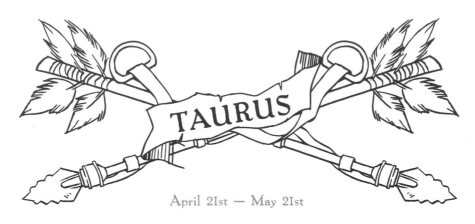

April 21st — May 21st

Unyielding in adversity.

_____
_____
_____
_____
_____
_____
_____
_____
_____
_____
_____
_____
_____
_____
_____
_____
_____
_____
_____
_____
_____
_____
_____
_____
_____
_____

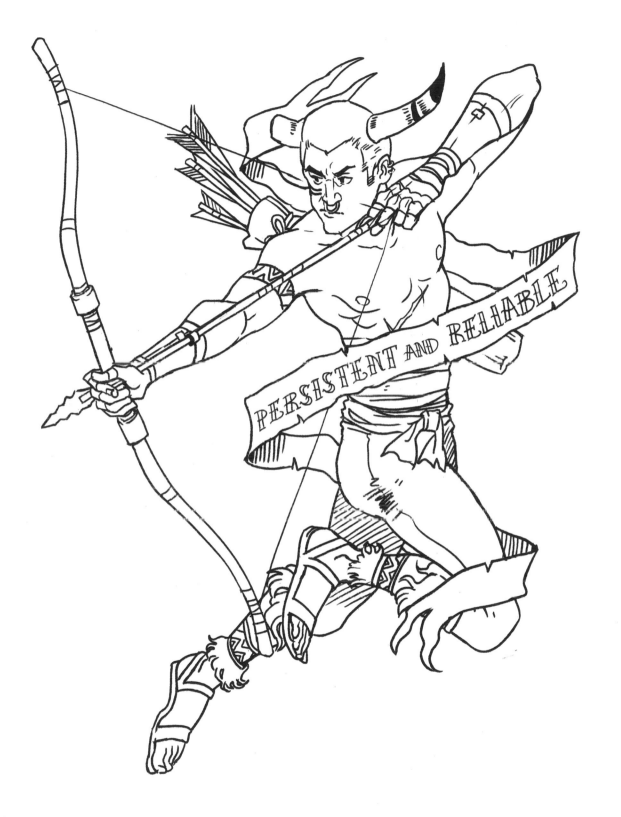

Gemini made their arrows so that they would avoid routine and boredom. Because the arrows are extremely thin, Gemini arrows are the only type that can be shot together; the number of arrows in each shot is always changing.

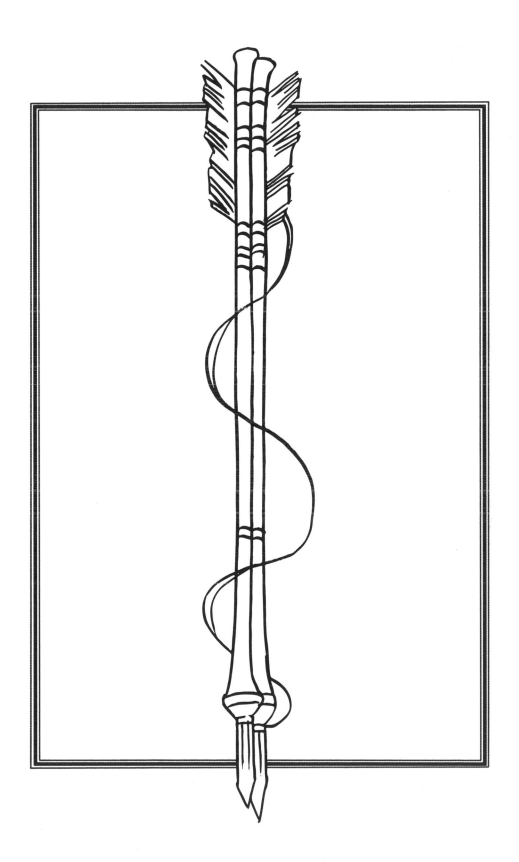

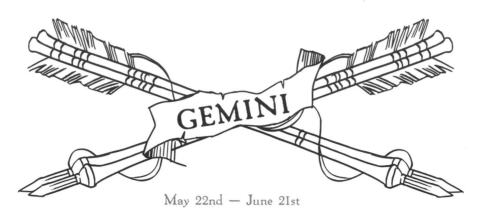

May 22nd — June 21st

Affection: a treasure most rare.

_____
_____
_____
_____
_____
_____
_____
_____
_____
_____
_____
_____
_____
_____
_____
_____
_____
_____
_____
_____
_____
_____
_____
_____
_____

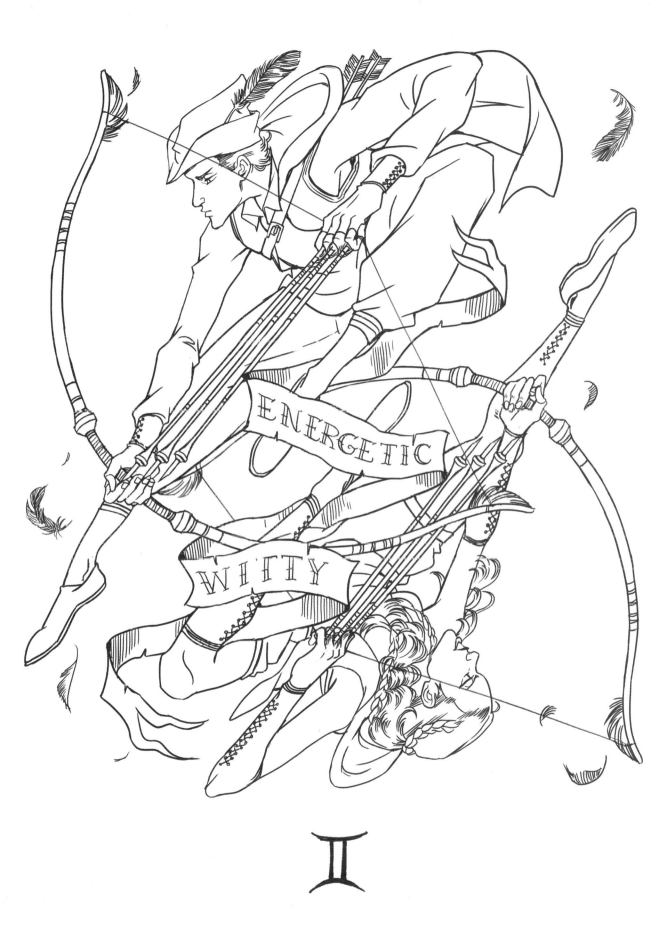

Cancer are deeply sensible and easily hurt so they designed their arrow in a way to avoid long fights. Their arrow is the most painful and cannot be removed.

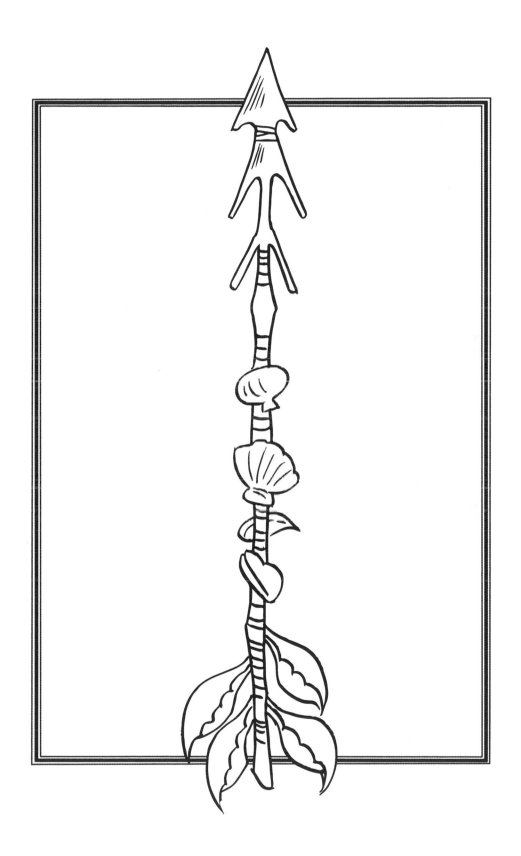

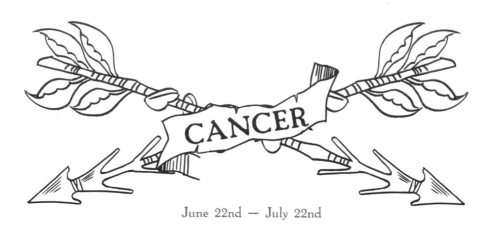

June 22nd — July 22nd

There is strength in tenacity.

_____
_____
_____
_____
_____
_____
_____
_____
_____
_____
_____
_____
_____
_____
_____
_____
_____
_____
_____
_____
_____
_____
_____
_____

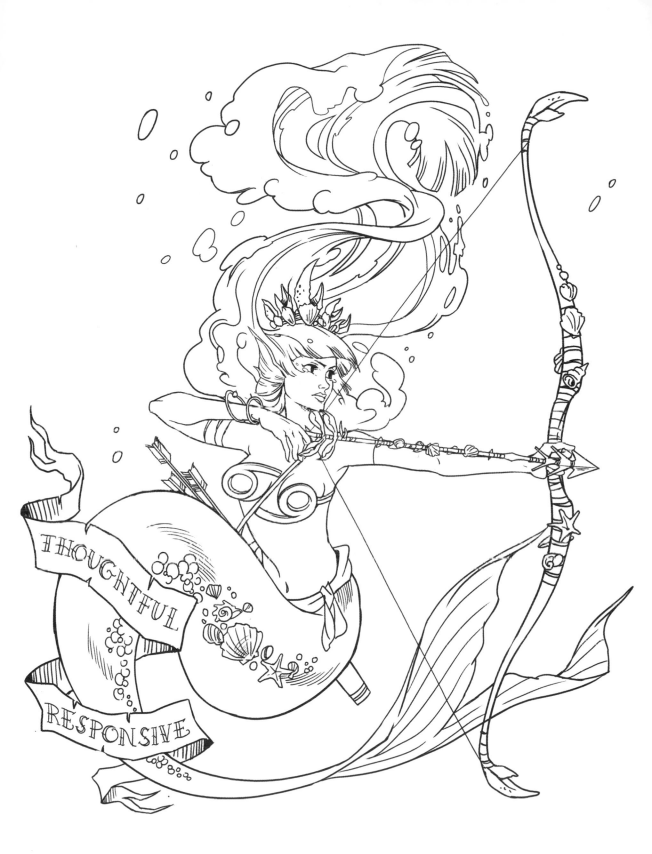

The fletching on a Leo's arrow is made from a lion's mane. The arrows are used to protect a Leo's kingdom—it may be anything, from home to a partner. Their jewels work as fuel for incendiary shots.

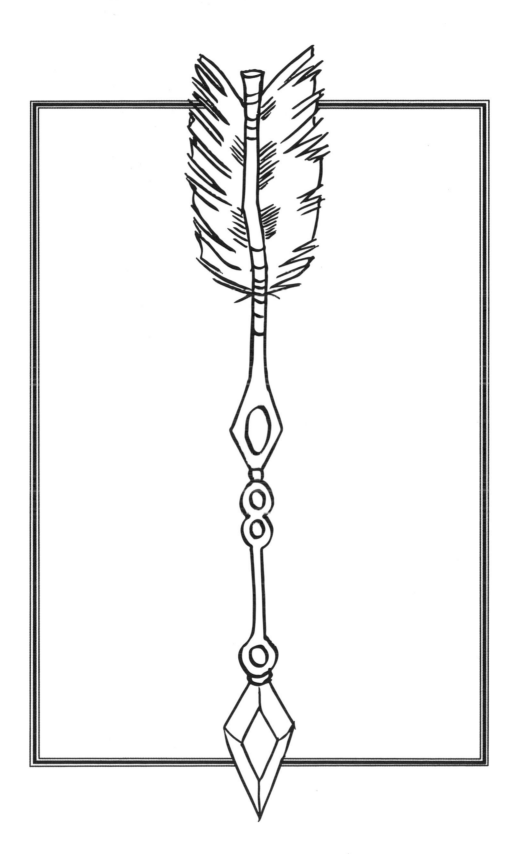

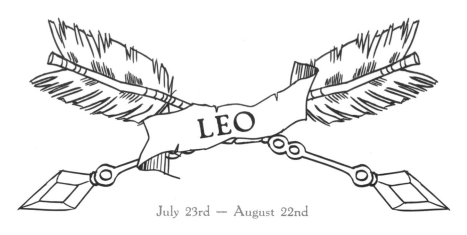

July 23rd — August 22nd

The creative fire does not consume.

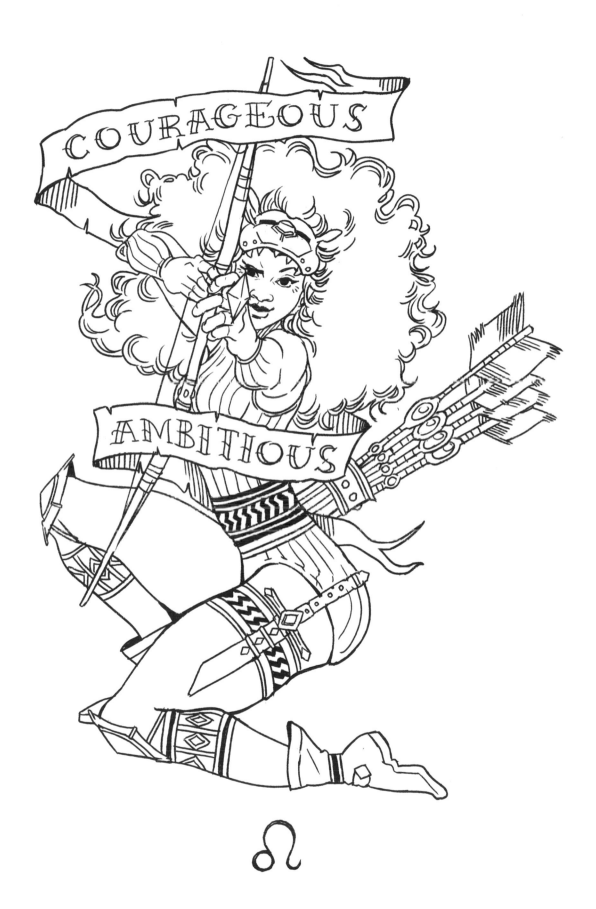

Virgo's perfectionism make them extremely picky about their enemies. Although their arrow seems delicate and calm on the outside, it only takes one shot to kill.

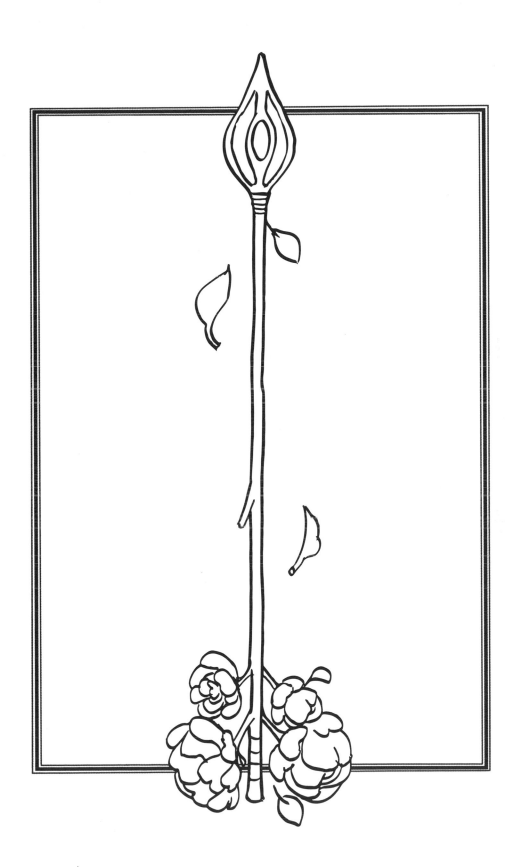

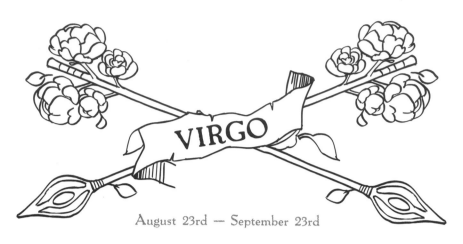

VIRGO

August 23rd — September 23rd

An arrow pulled back is an arrow ready to fire.

_____
_____
_____
_____
_____
_____
_____
_____
_____
_____
_____
_____
_____
_____
_____
_____
_____
_____
_____
_____
_____
_____
_____

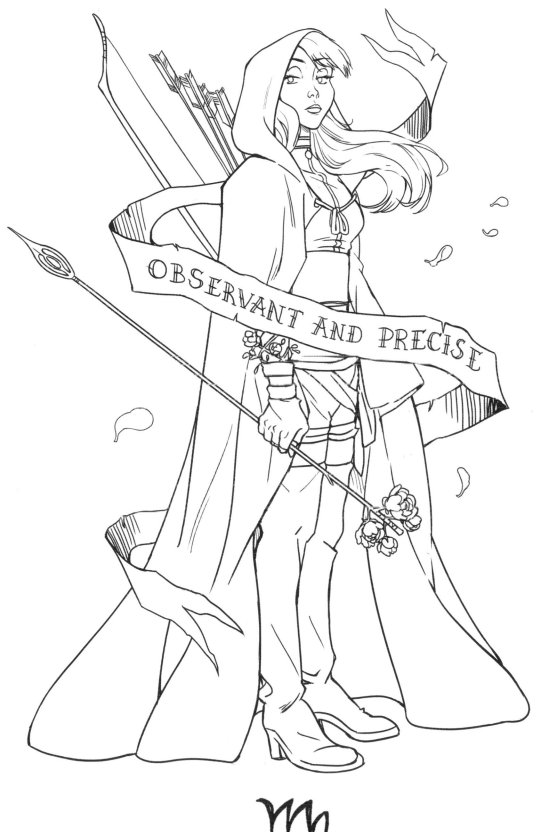

Libra are the diplomats of the zodiac. Their arrow's tip resembles the pans in the scales of Justice. Just like "Justice is blind," so is the arrow's tip. It is meant to end fights, not be part of them.

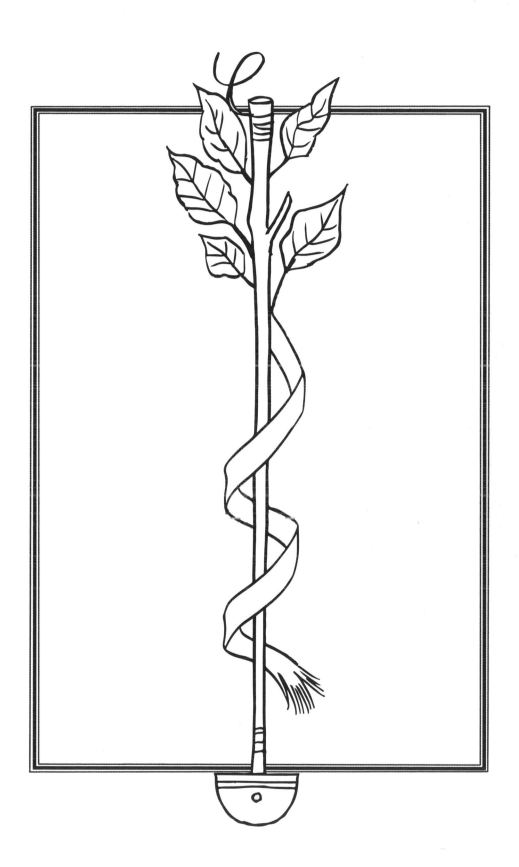

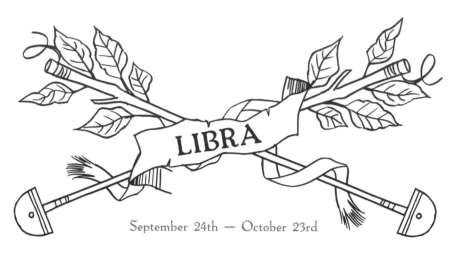

LIBRA

September 24th — October 23rd

Diplomacy is the art of letting
somebody else have your way.

_____

_____

_____

_____

_____

_____

_____

_____

_____

_____

_____

_____

_____

_____

_____

_____

_____

_____

_____

_____

_____

_____

_____

_____

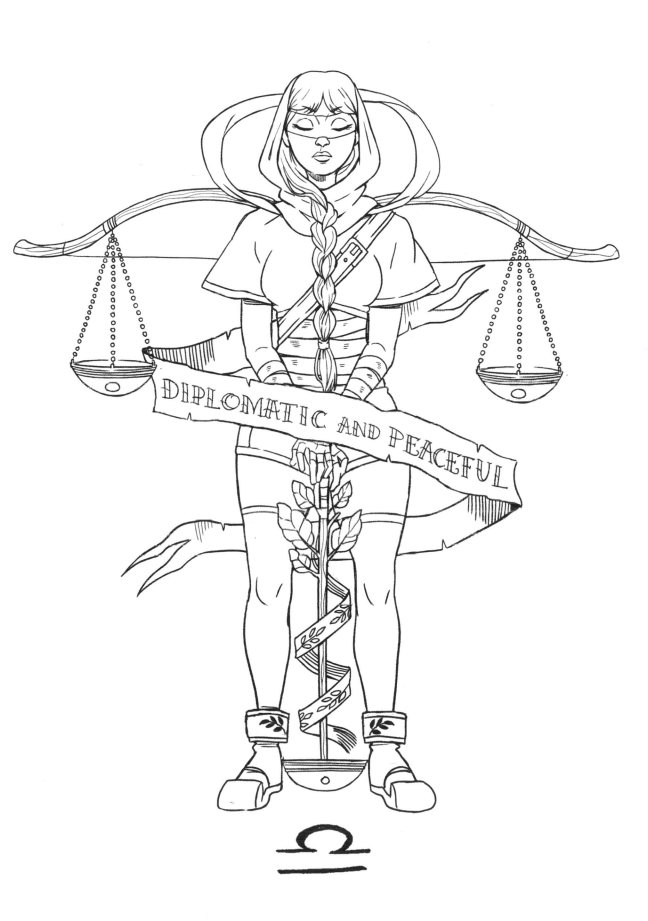

Scorpio have the tail of a scorpion on their arrow's tip, which is poisonous and can kill their victim slowly. Scorpio have a natural secretiveness so they choose not to change their arrow's fletching. After piercing an enemy in battle, it's hard to tell if said arrow came from a Scorpio.

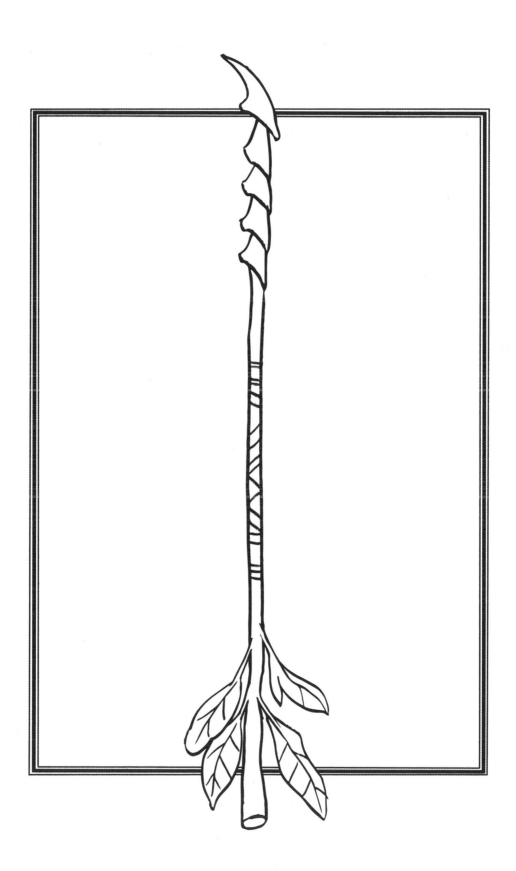

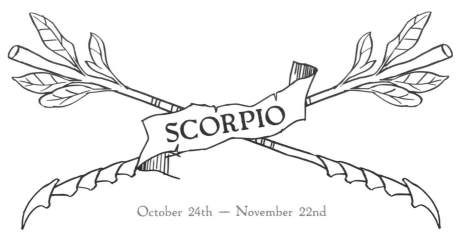

SCORPIO

October 24th — November 22nd

There is no bravery in being
consumed with distrust.

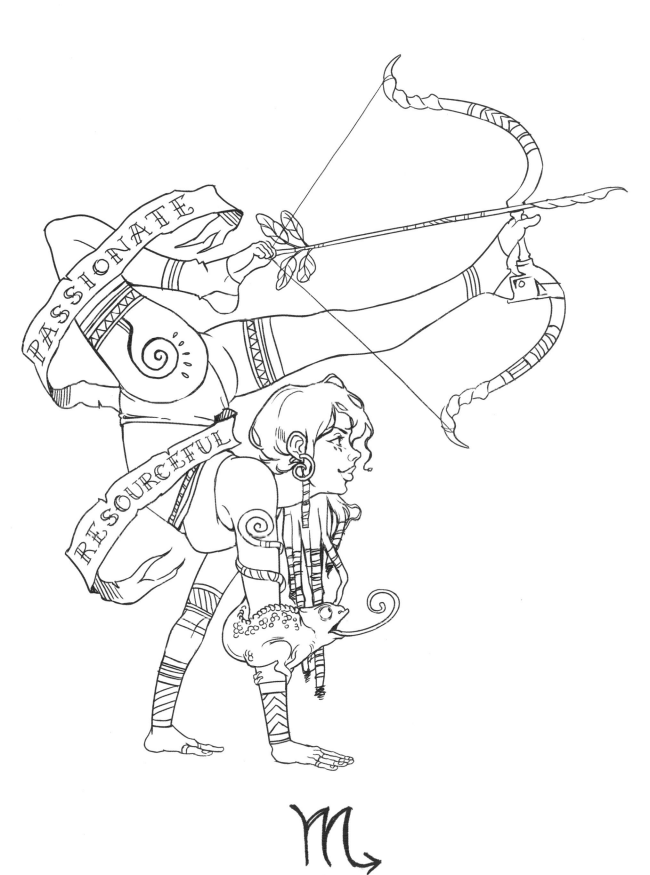

Sagittarius' were not influenced by Aries' custom arrows. As natural archers, Sagittarius' arrows were always the shape of their zodiac sign. These arrows can travel unbelievable distances, and are often mistaken for shooting stars.

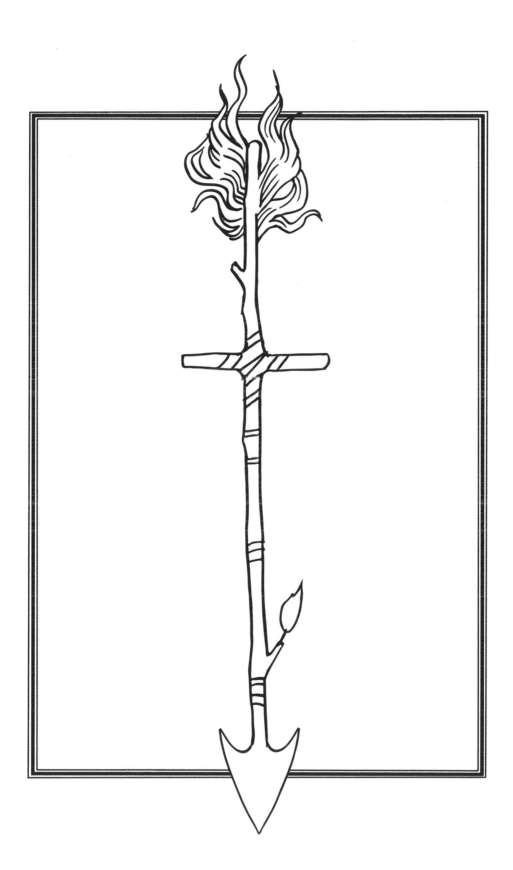

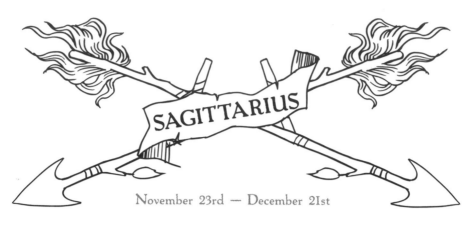

November 23rd — December 21st

Freedom is the greatest treasure.

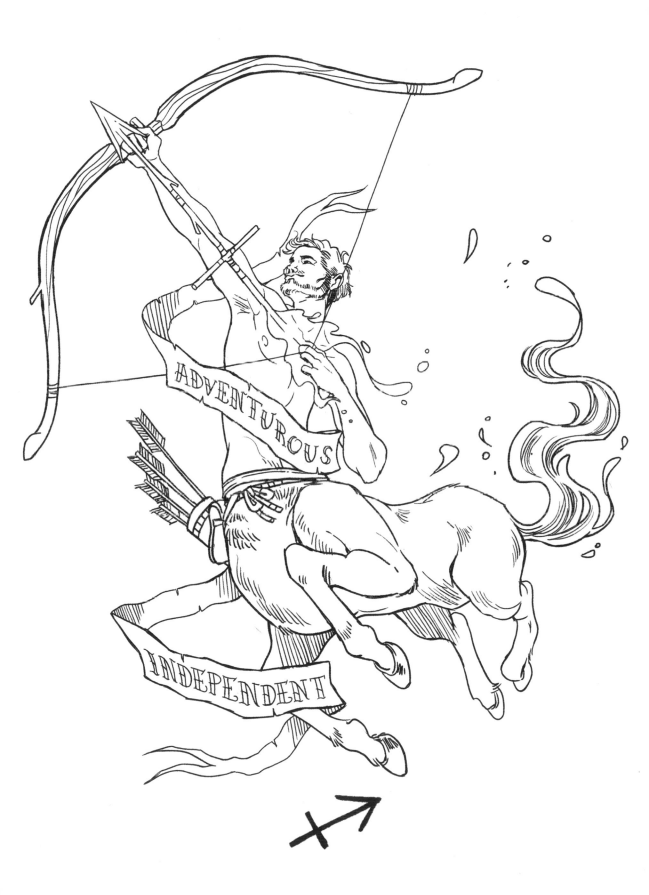

Capricorns have always been resistant to big changes so they decided to modify their arrow only once and never again. The fish tail in the place of the fletching is reminiscent of their sign symbol, a sea goat. It can change the direction of the arrow after being shot, making this arrow impossible to escape.

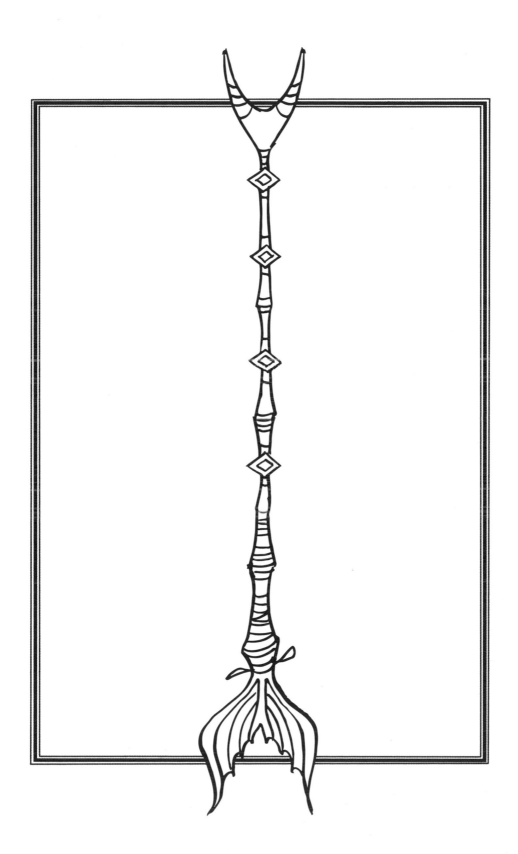

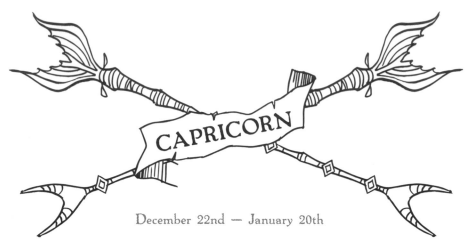

CAPRICORN

December 22nd — January 20th

Leadership is emboldened by the enrichment of self.

_____
_____
_____
_____
_____
_____
_____
_____
_____
_____
_____
_____
_____
_____
_____
_____
_____
_____
_____
_____
_____
_____
_____

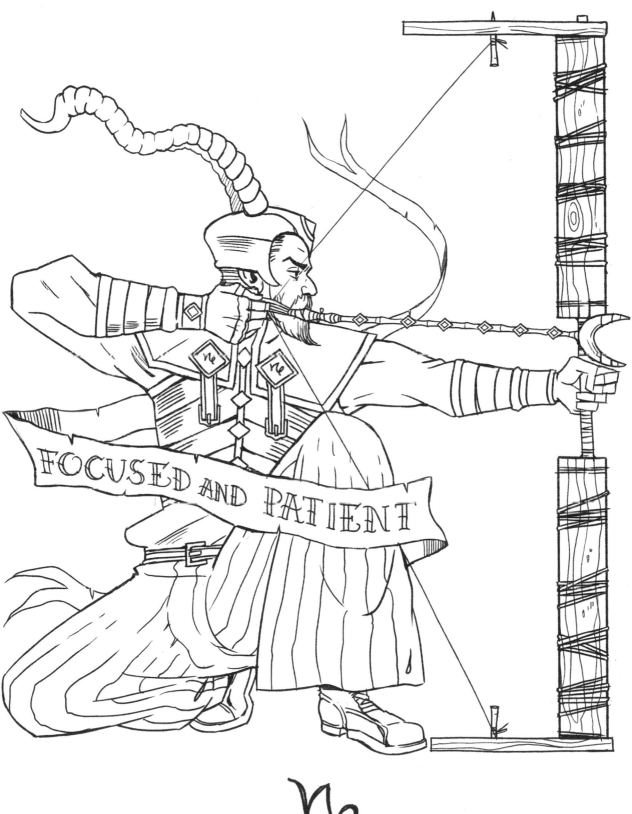

Aquarius' are known for their inventiveness and originality. They improved the arrows transportation forever, instead of a quiver their magic arrows are carried on a water bearer which resembles their sign symbol. To pick their arrow, they pour it from the bearer.

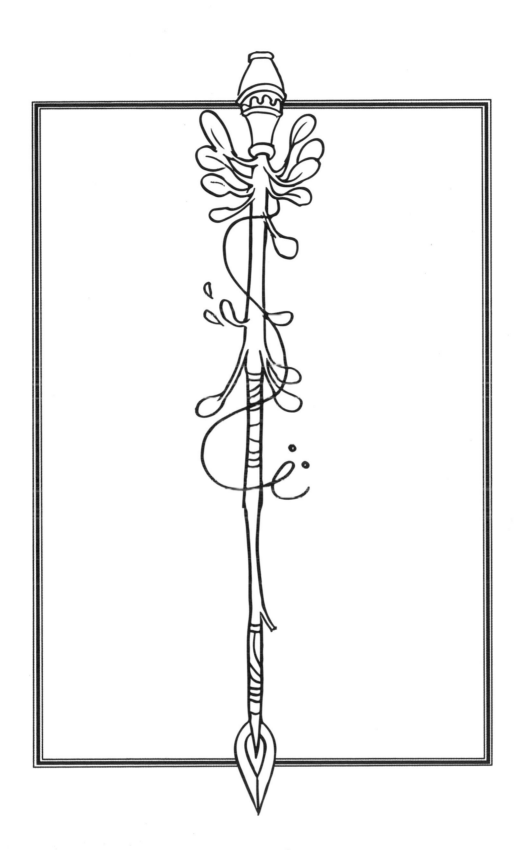

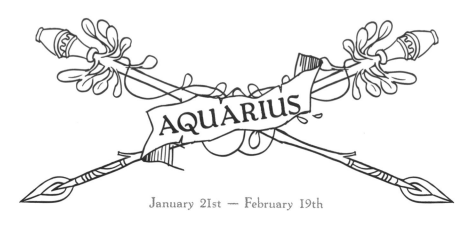

AQUARIUS

January 21st — February 19th

Growth is the flowering of meager triumphs.

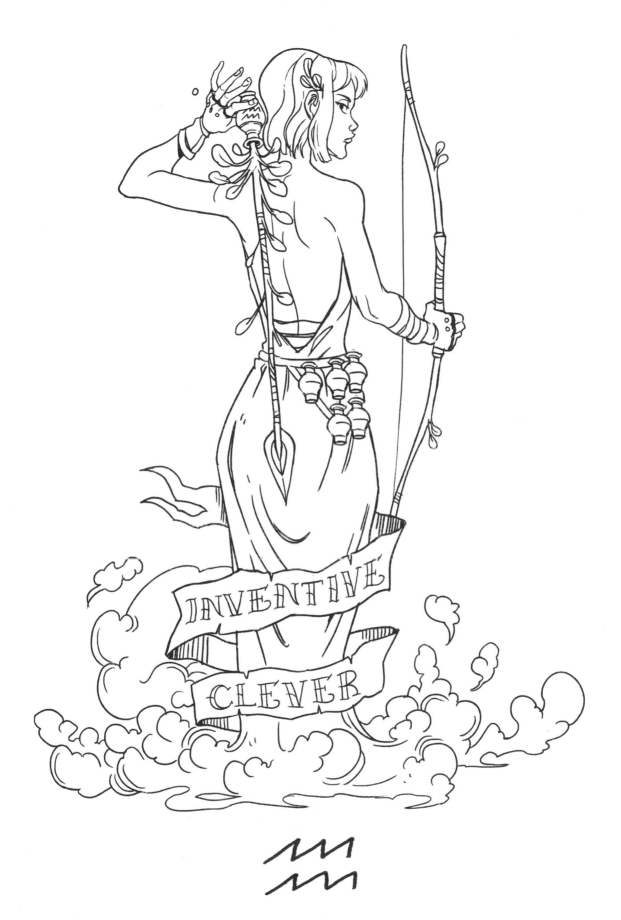

Pisces' arrows were the last to be created. As Pisces is the sign of mysticism and spirituality, their arrows are capable of piercing the souls of their enemies. Much of this arrow's characteristics are unknown.

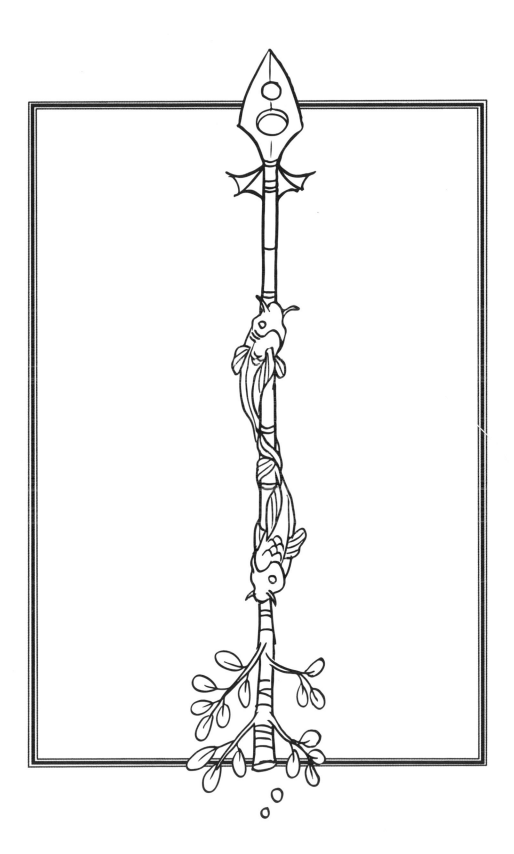

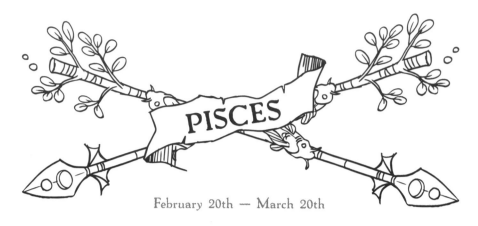

PISCES

February 20th — March 20th

Empathy is the pillar of strength.

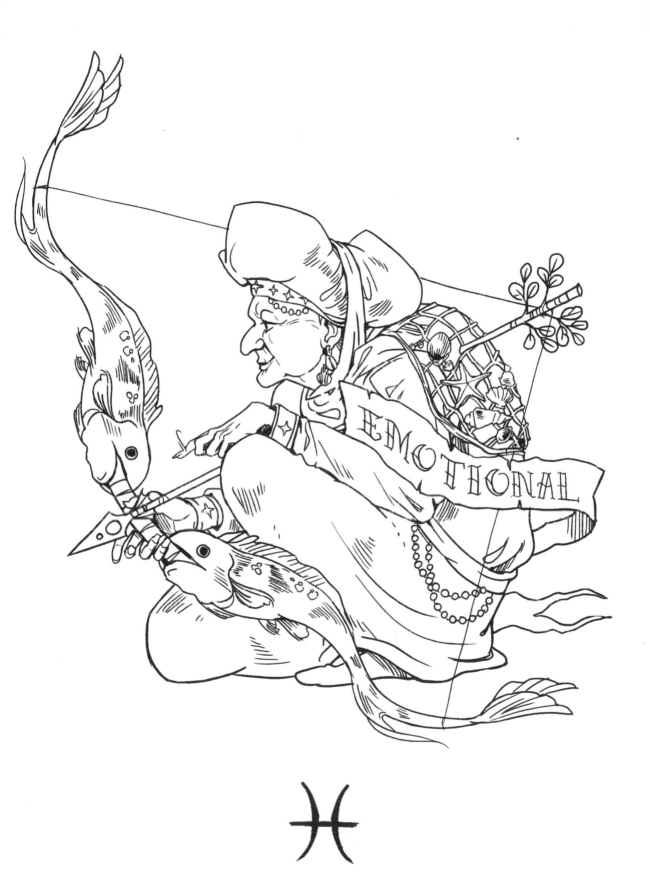

Look up at the stars when you
feel alone in this Universe;

Some of them might just
feel the same.

The Chameleon likes to camouflage
itself on the night sky, so that it can't
be found by the naked eye. It is
the keeper of the Scorpio arrow.

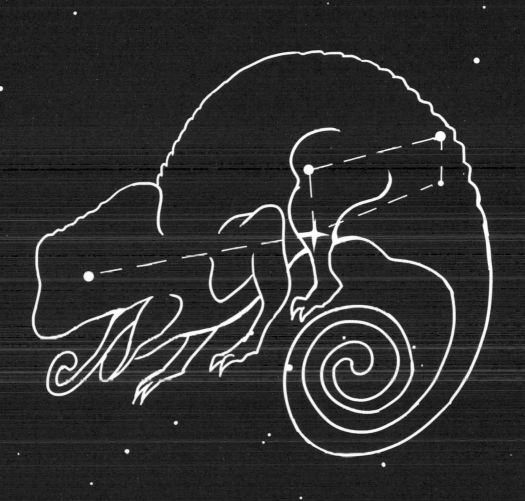

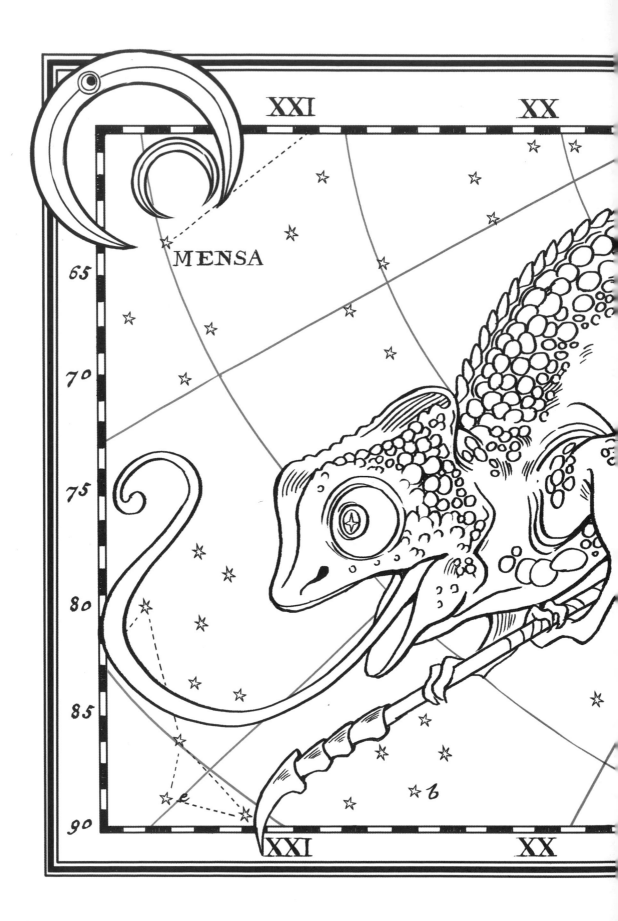

MENSA

65

70

75

80

85

90

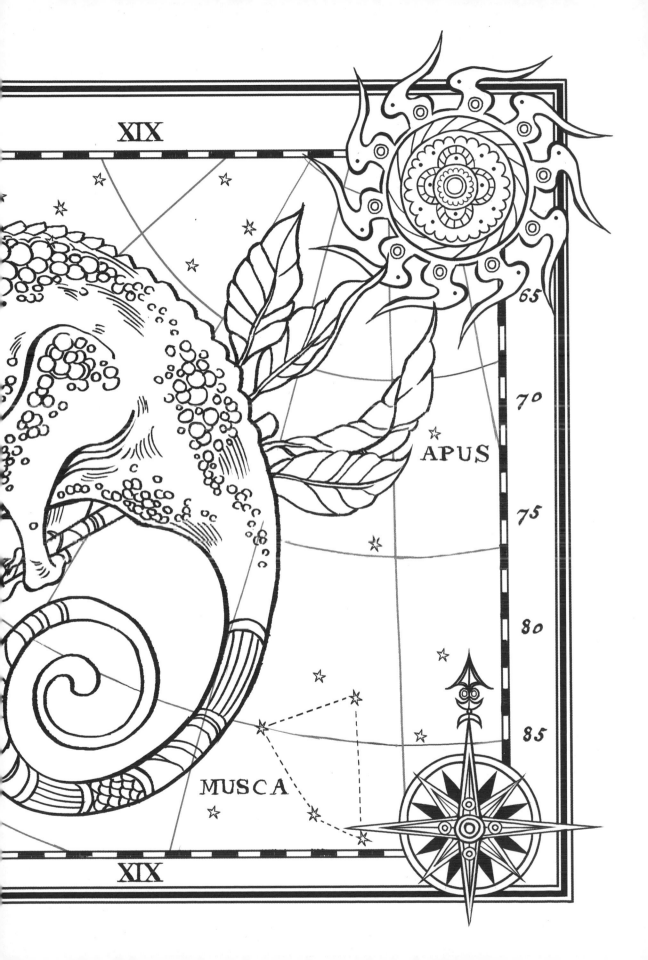

65

70

APUS

75

80

85

MUSCA

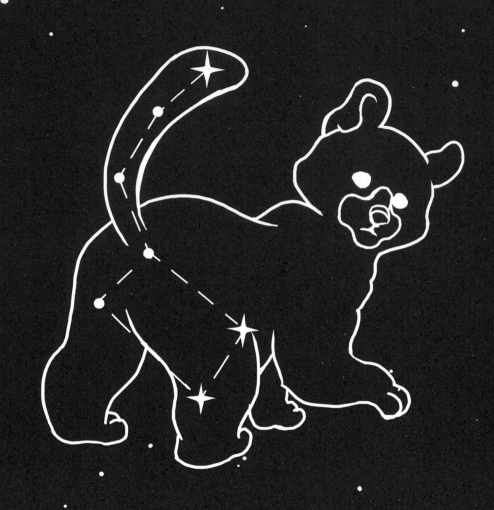

Ursa Major and Ursa Minor were mother and son transformed into bears, grabbed by their tails, and swung into the heavens to live amongst the stars.

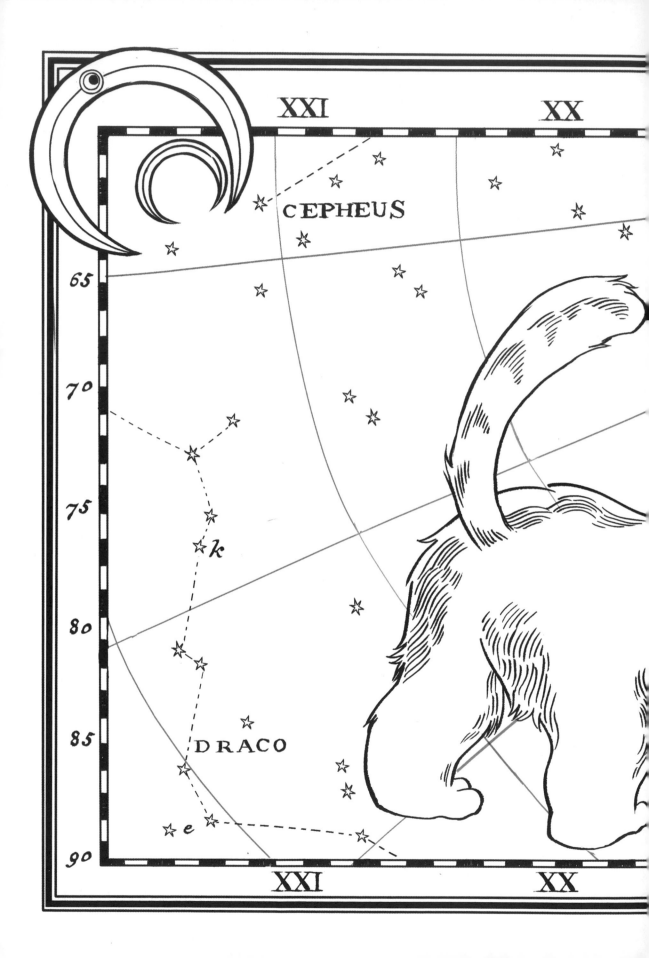

CEPHEUS

65

70

75

k

80

85

DRACO

e

90

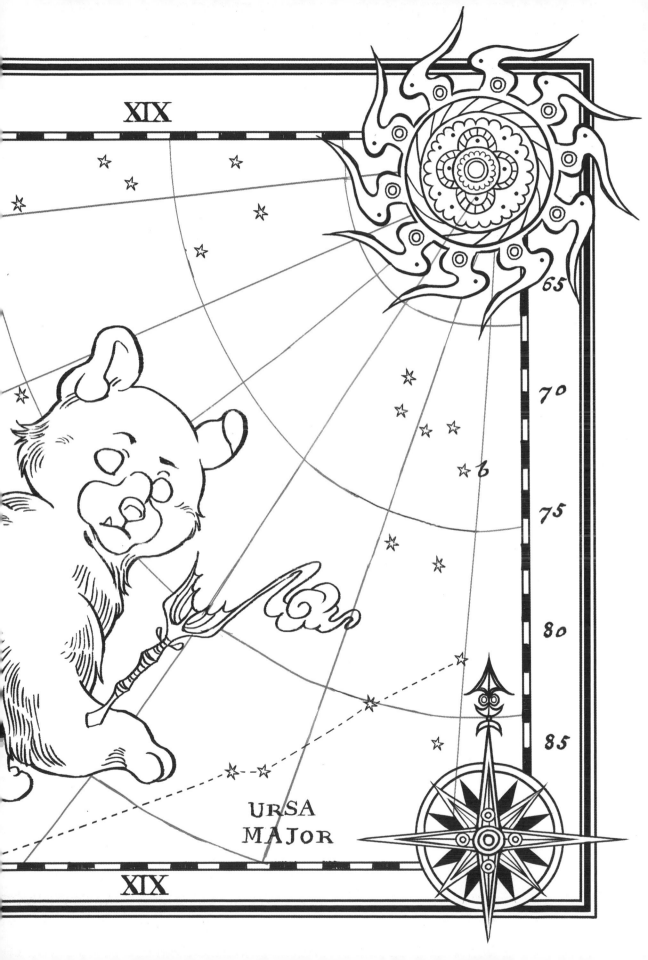

XIX

65

70

6

75

80

85

URSA
MAJor

XIX

Legend has it that Lepus once escaped
the Capricorn arrow; the one that is said
to never miss its target.

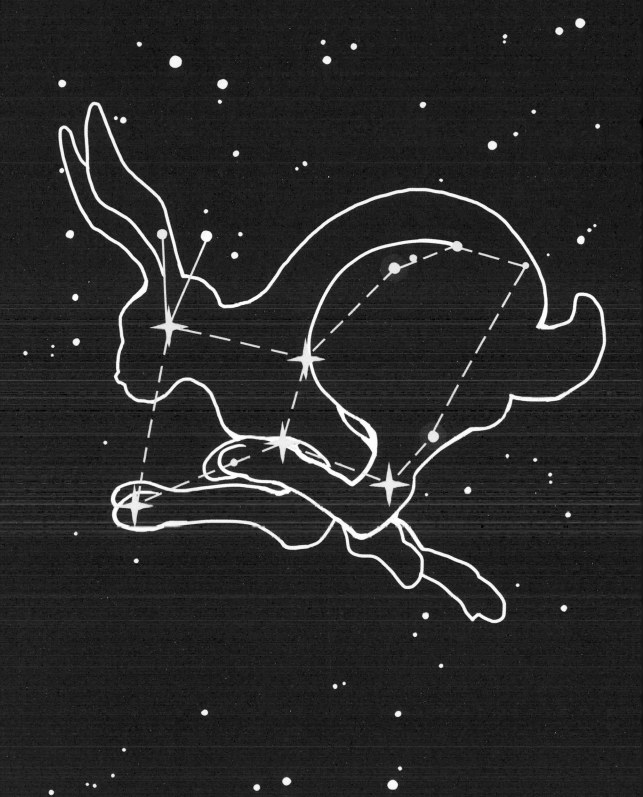

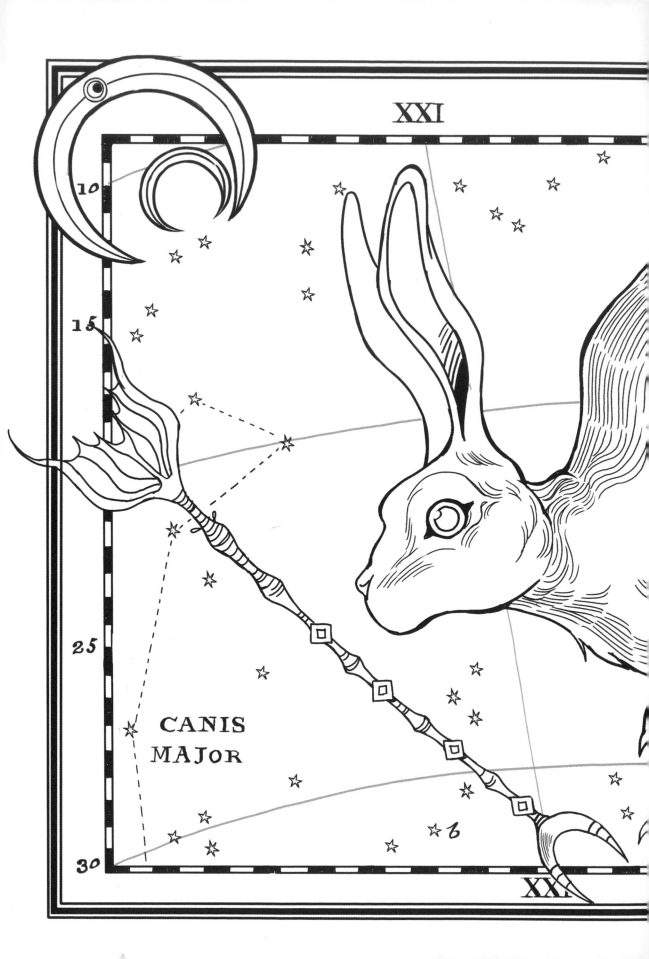

10

15

25

CANIS
MAJOR

30

*6

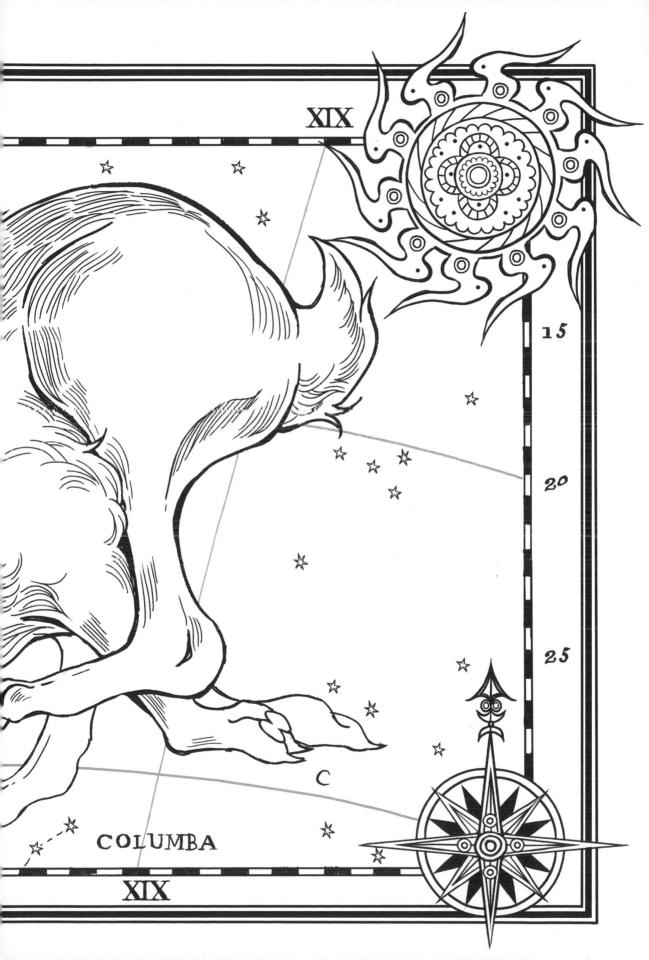

15

20

25

C

COLUMBA

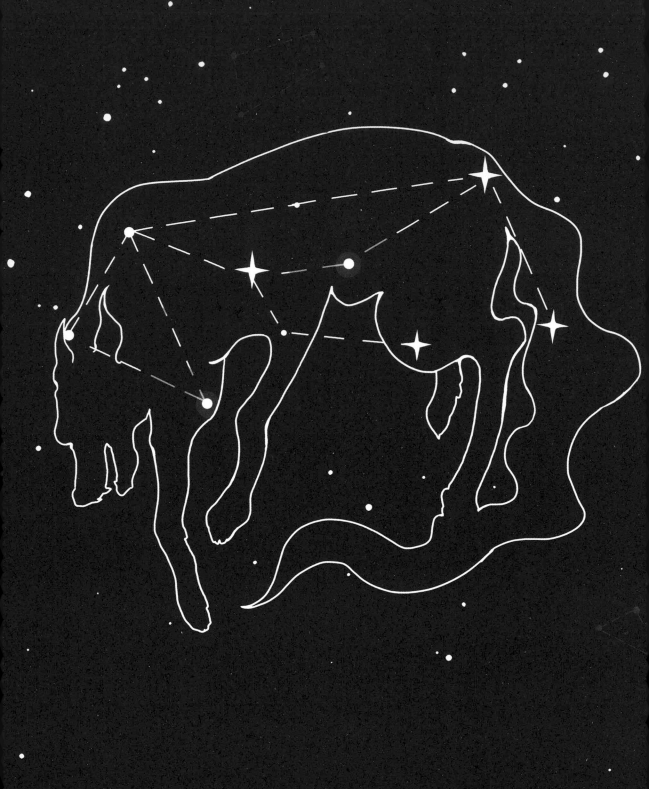

Lupus is agile, swift, and a ferocious hunter. It is said that Lupus can sense foul intentions.

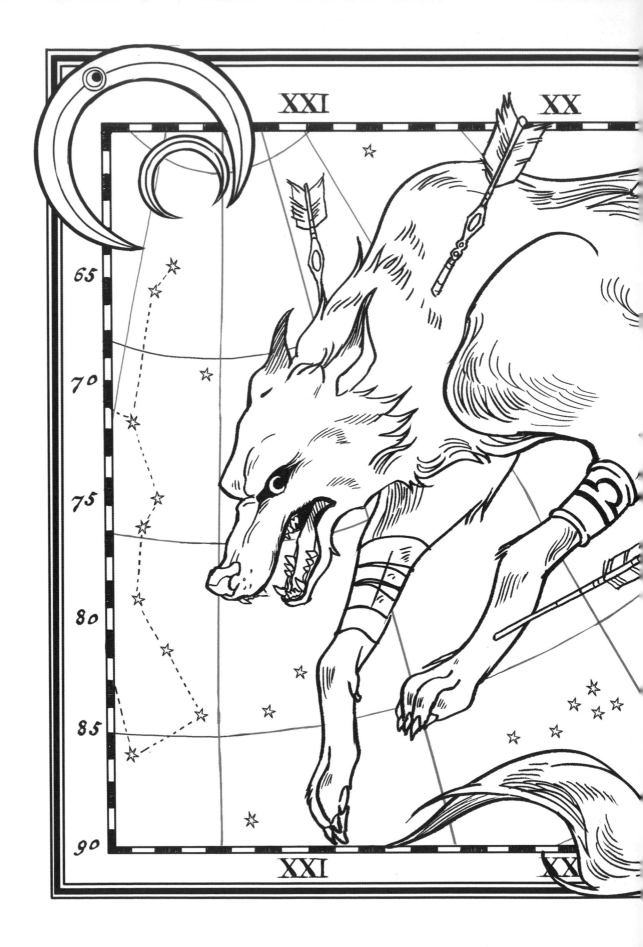

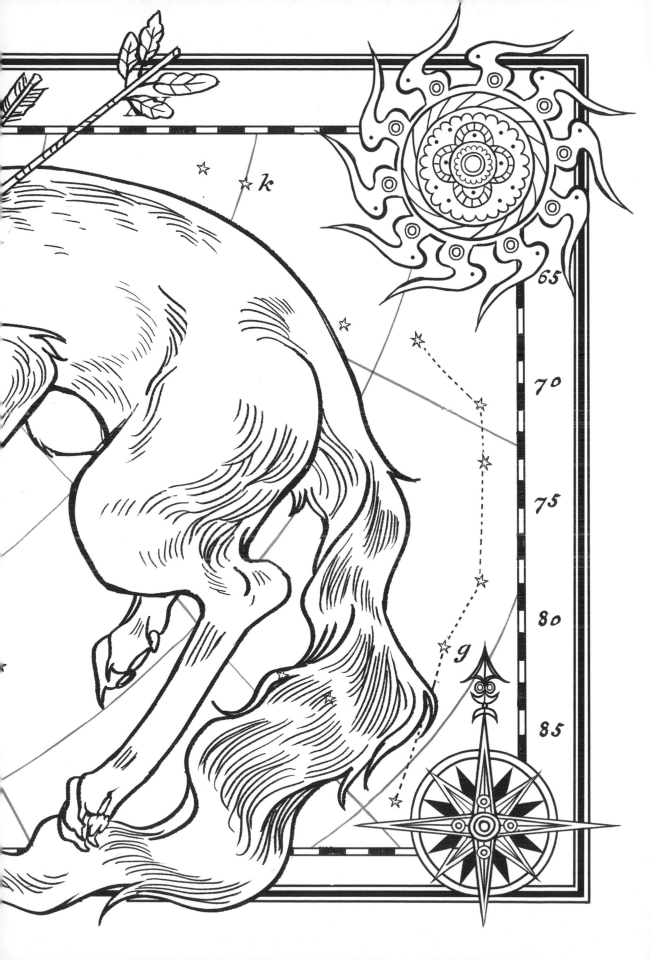

k

65

70

75

80

g

85

Cygnus is a noble constellation that rules the northern hemisphere of the night sky. She is believed to be the keeper of Pisces' arrows.

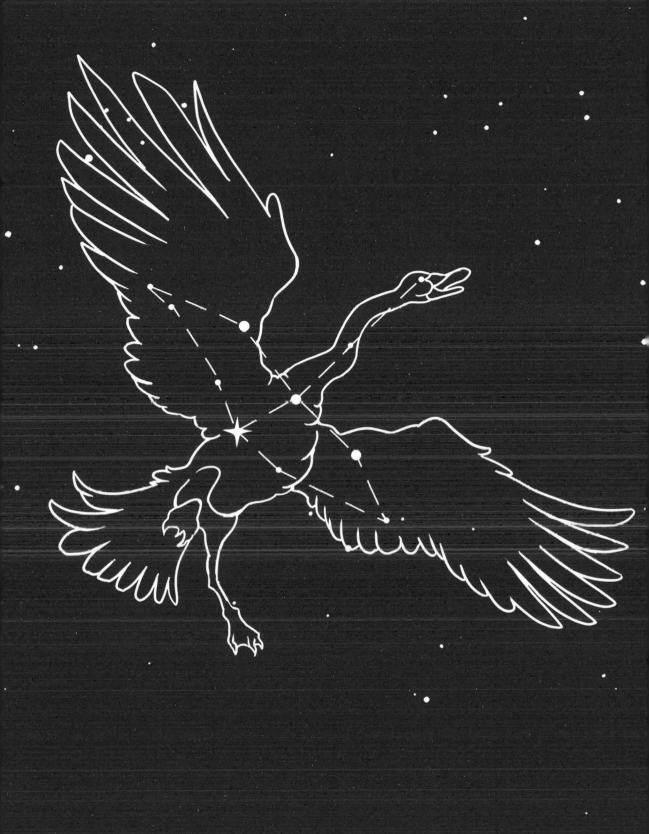

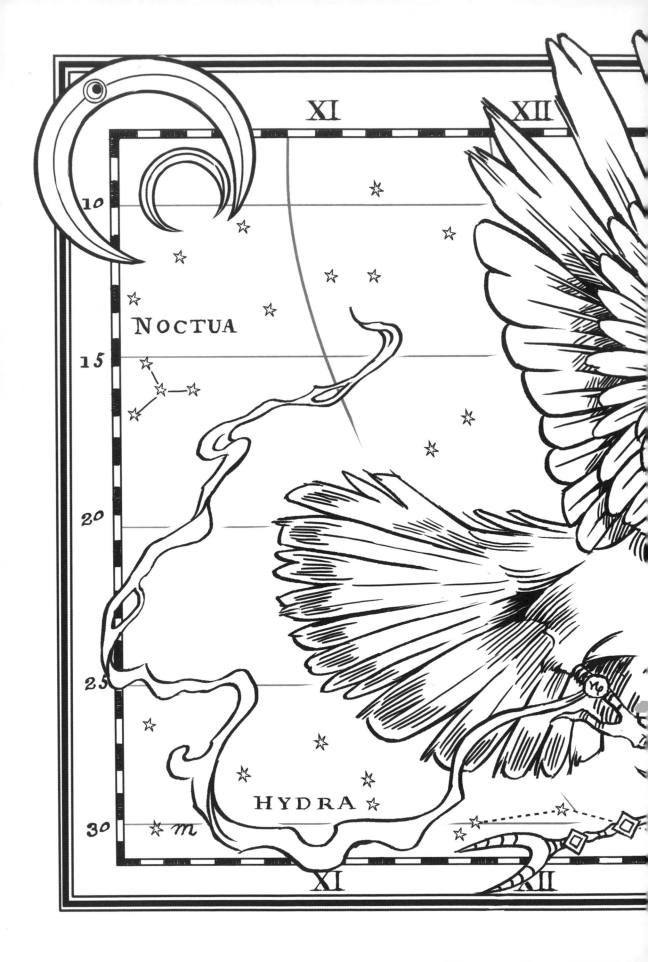

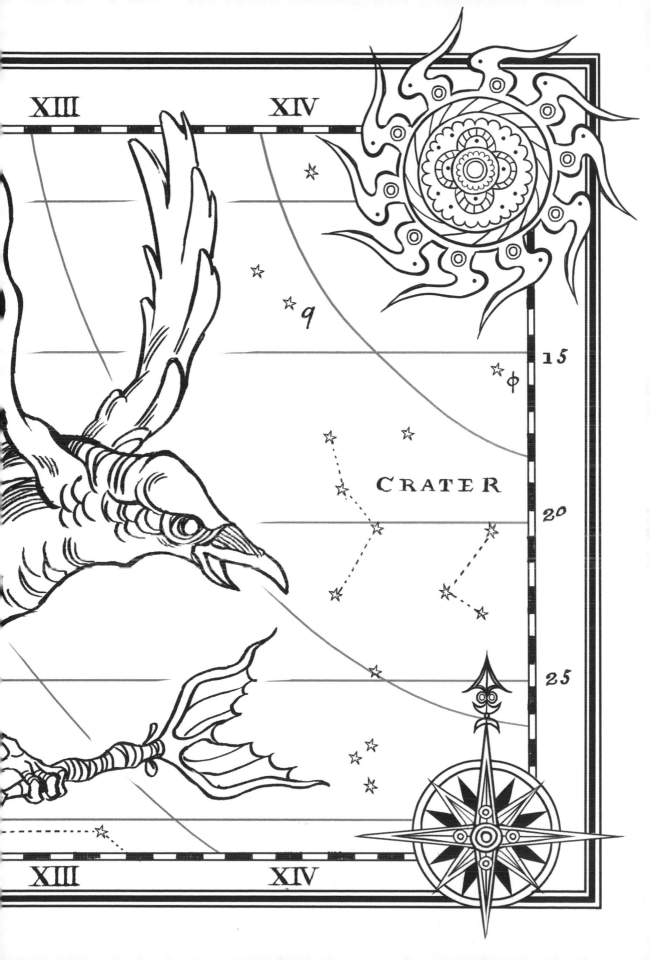

9

15

φ

CRATER

20

25

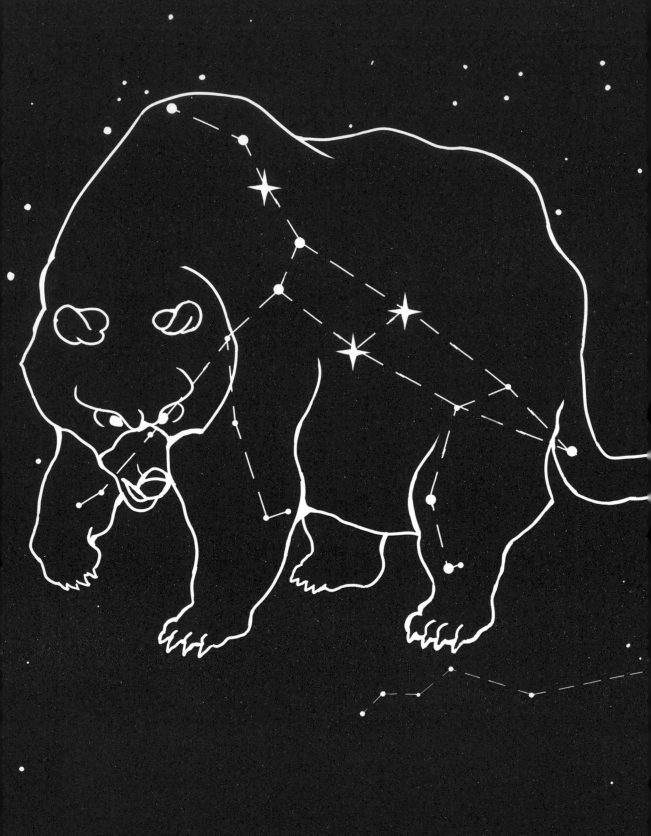

Ursa Major is one of the oldest constellations in the sky. Her roar sounds like desert thunder and she has the wisdom of thousands of years gone by.

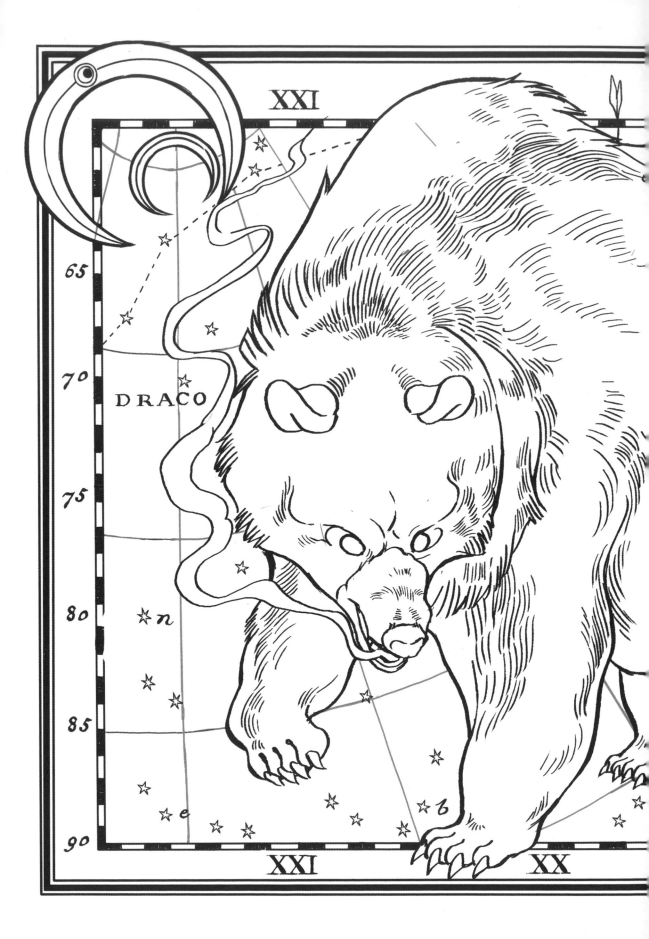

65

70°

DRACO

75

80

85

90

n

e

b

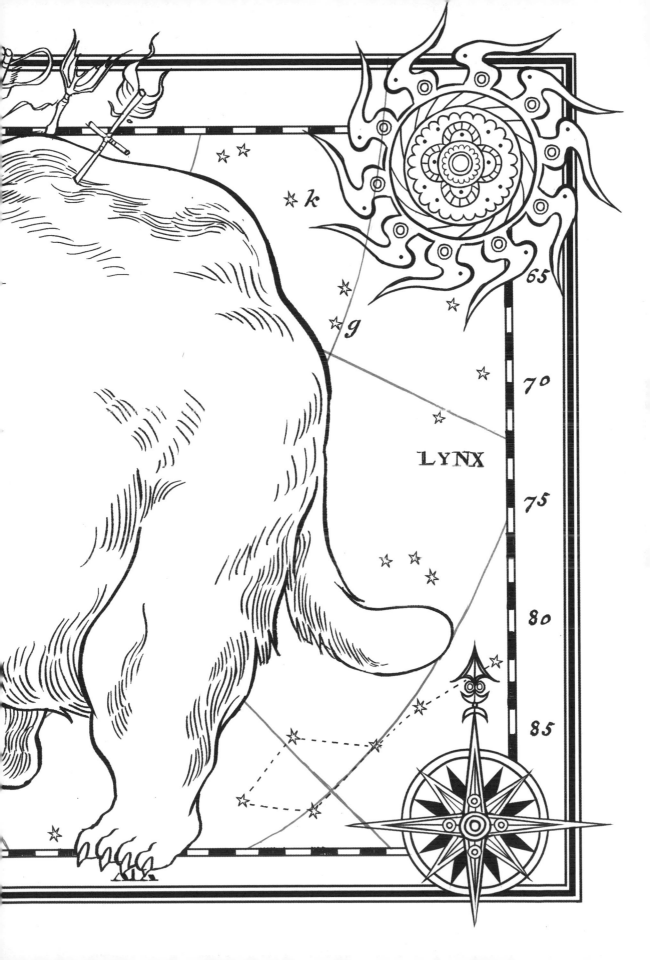

k

g

65

70

LYNX

75

80

85

XIX

Vulpecula travel the sky alone; running their own errands. They're also keepers of Sagittarius' arrows.

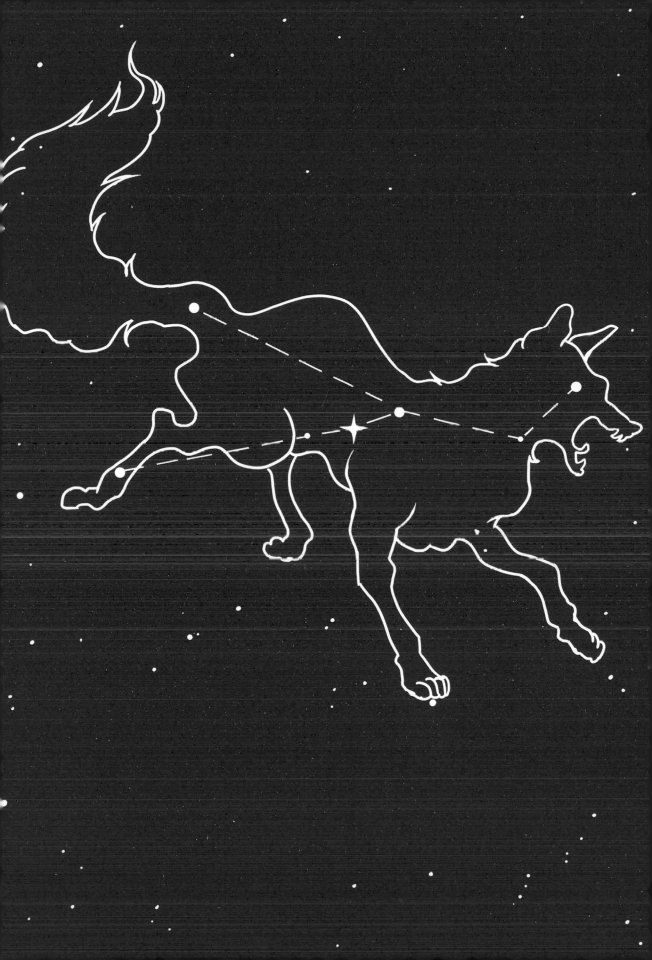

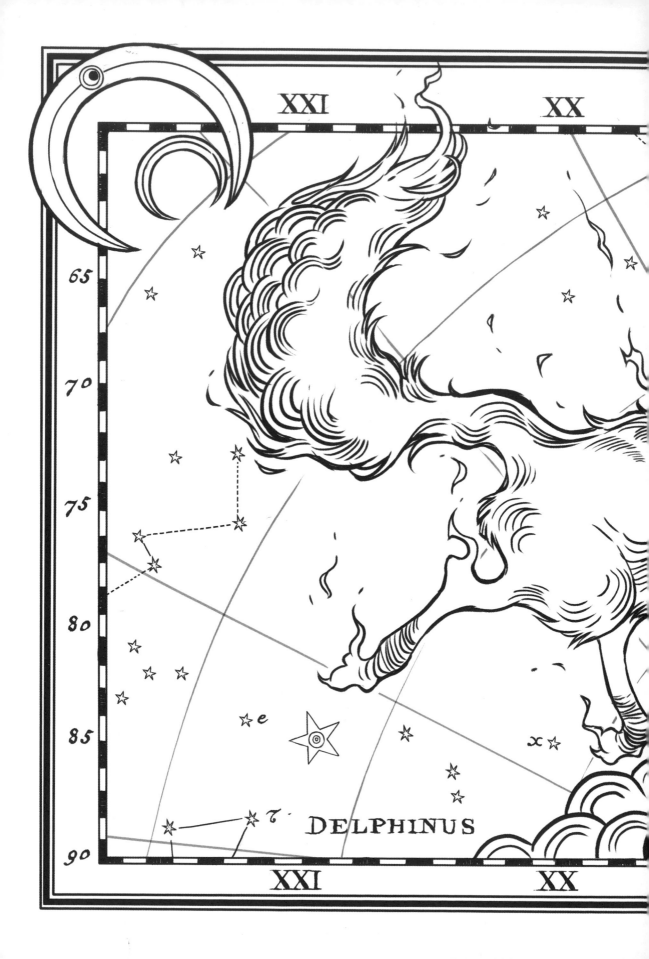

65

70

75

80

85

e

x

90

δ DELPHINUS

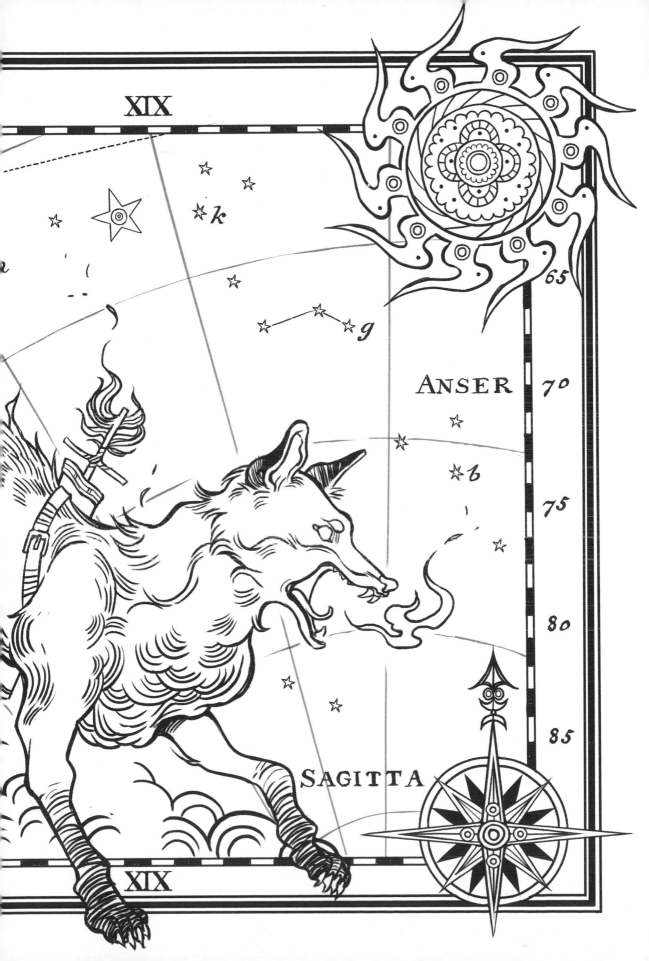

*k

g

ANSER

65

70

*b

75

80

SAGITTA

85

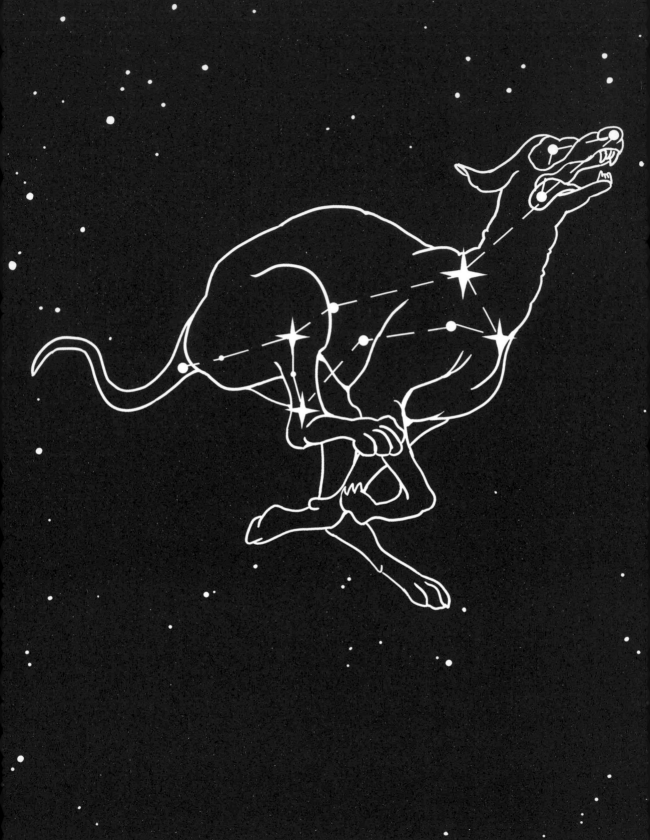

Canis Major shines with its vitality and excitement. It is one of the brightest constellations in the night sky. It is also keeper of Gemini's arrows.

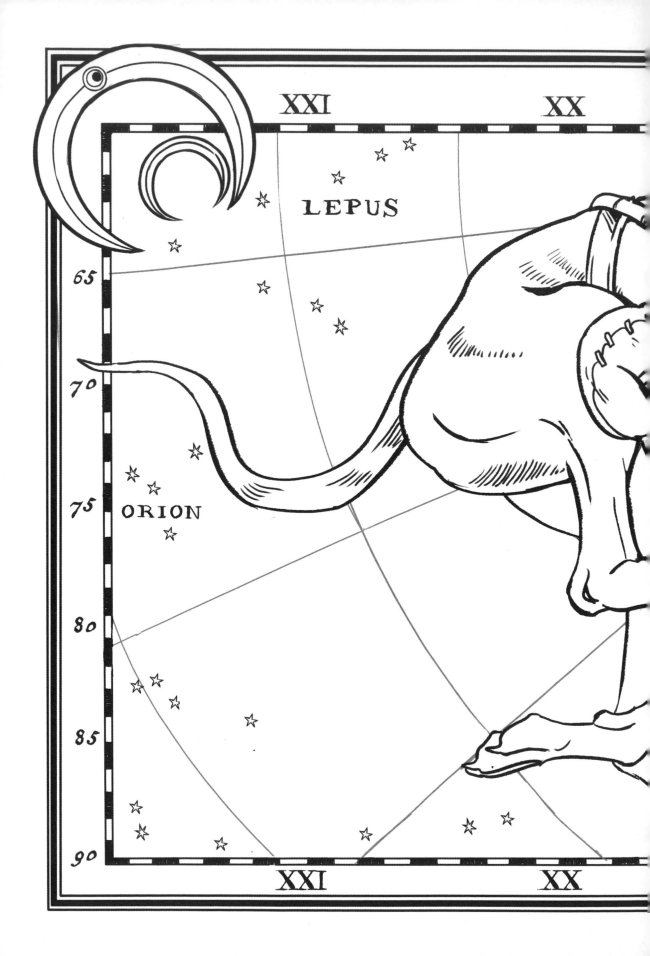

LEPUS

65

70

ORION

75

80

85

90

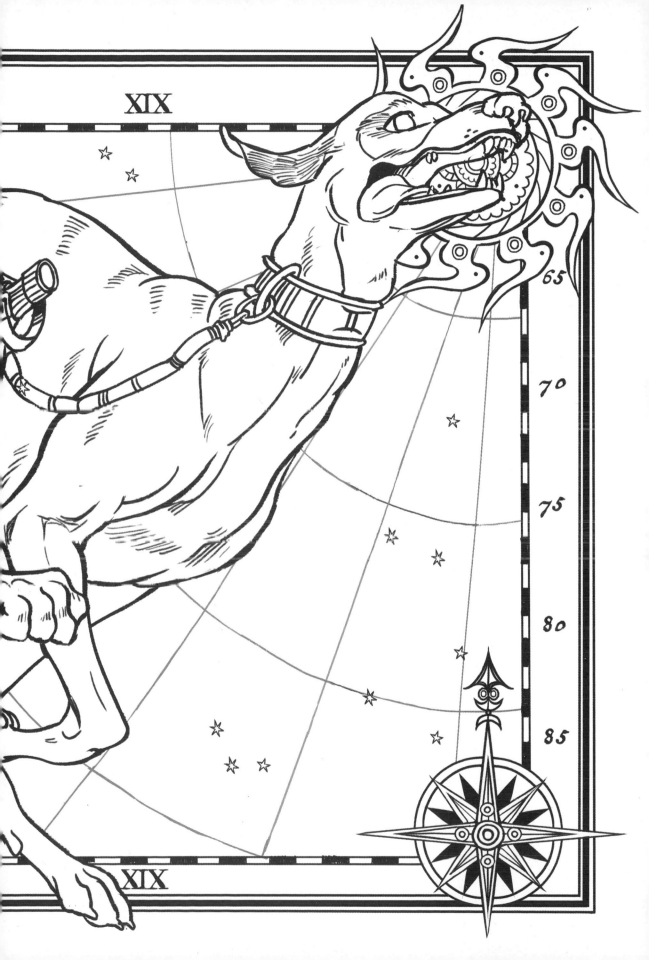

65

70

75

80

85

Pavo is believed to draw impurities from
its surroundings and incorporate them
into its many feathers and colors.

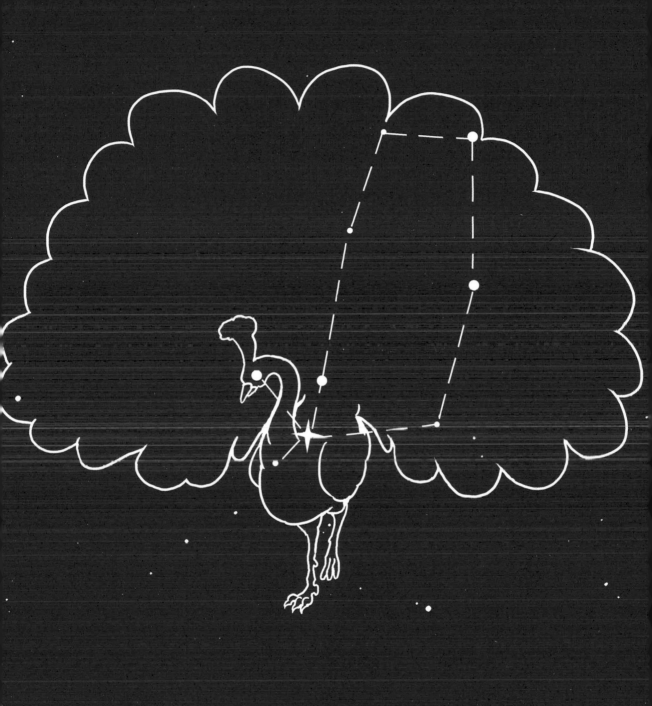

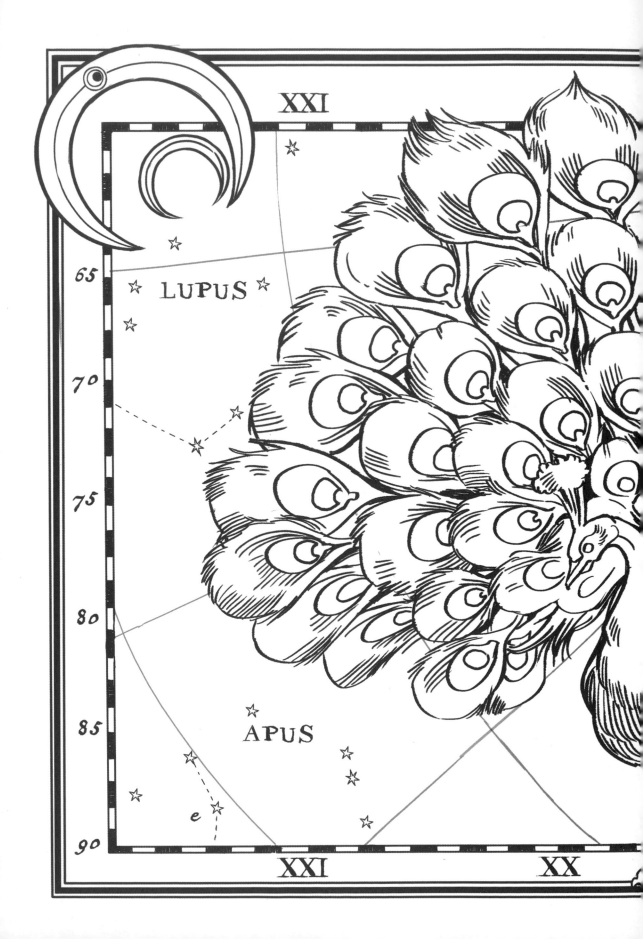

65

LUPUS

70

75

80

85

APuS

90

e

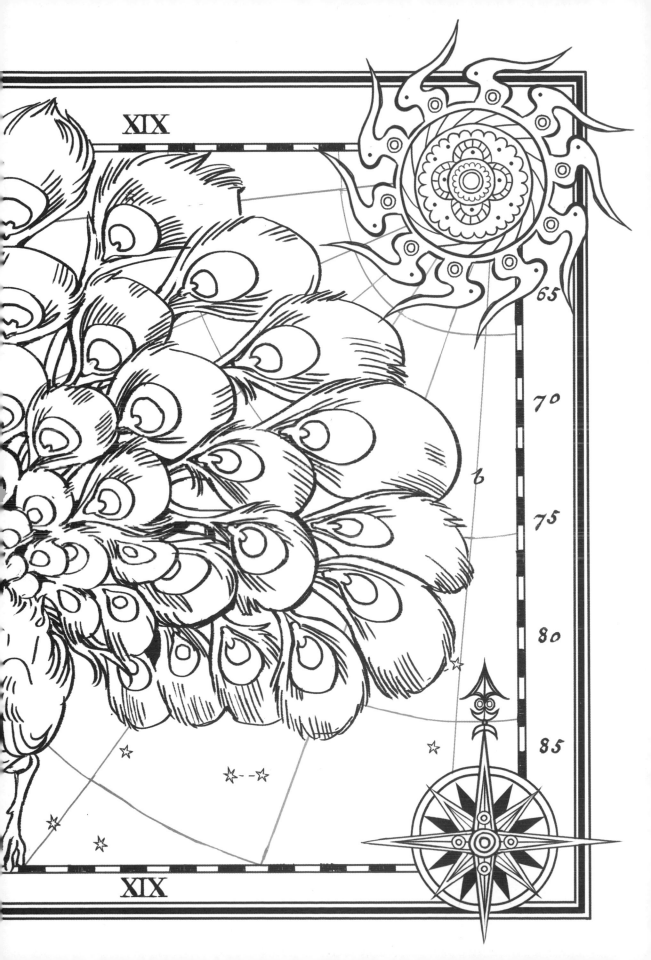

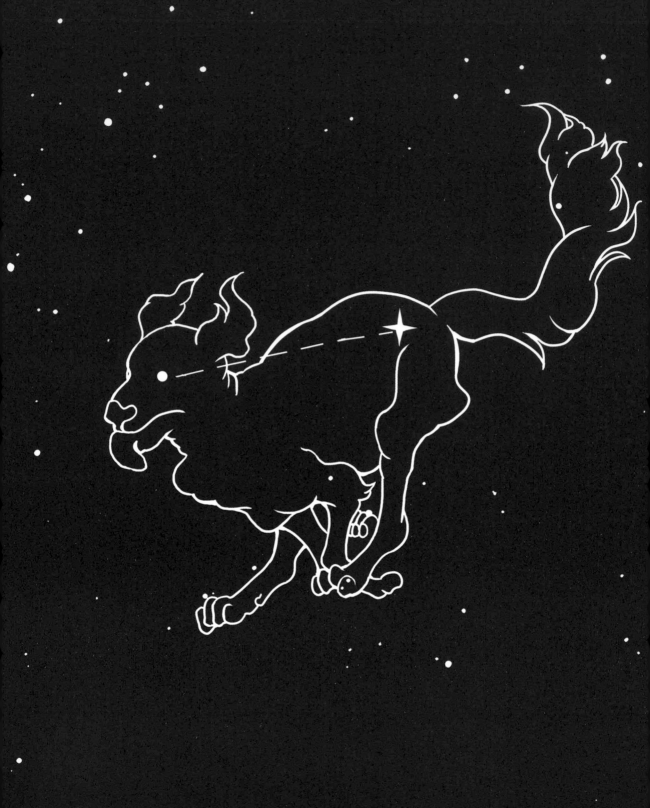

Canis Minor is the loyal companion of Canis Major. This constellation is very stubborn and it became the keeper of Gemini's arrows so that it could stay close to Canis Major.

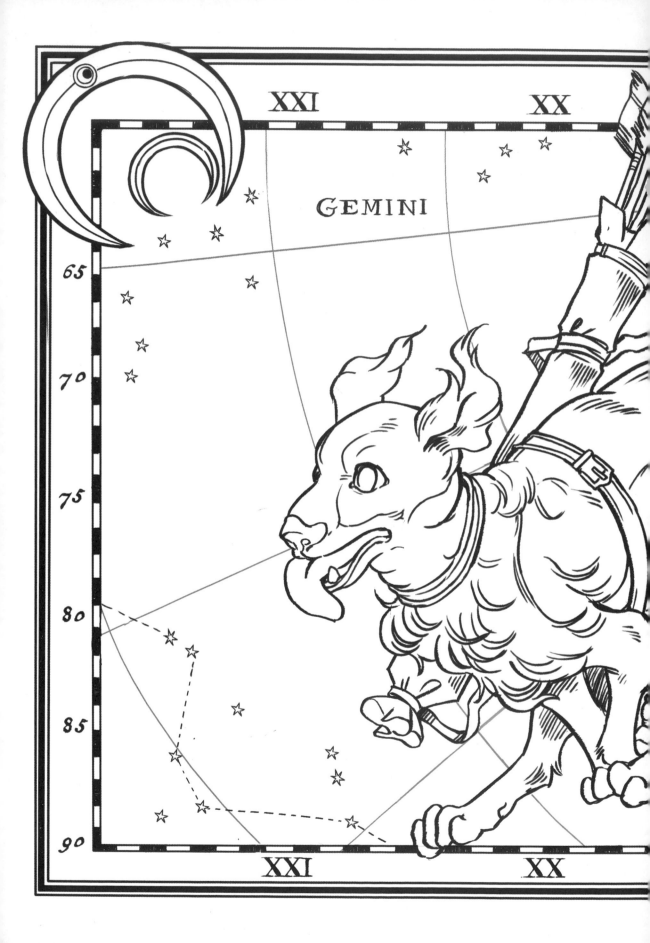

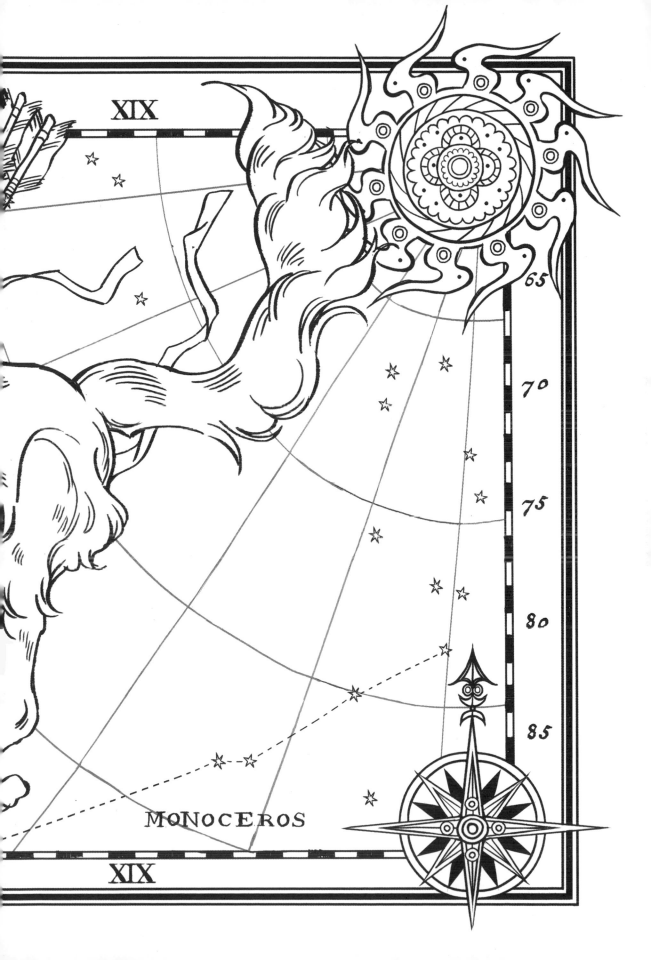

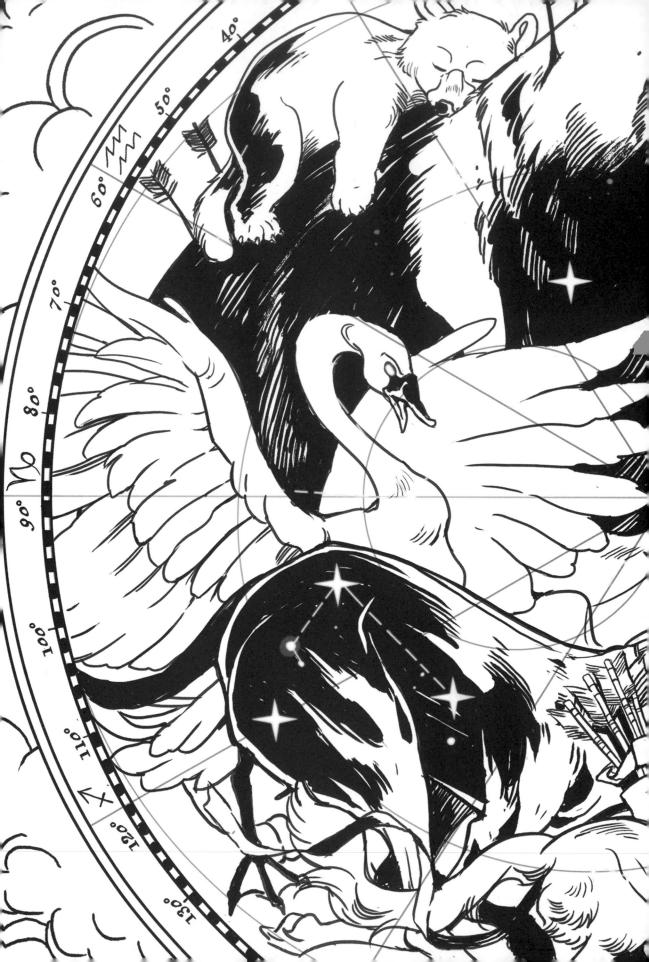

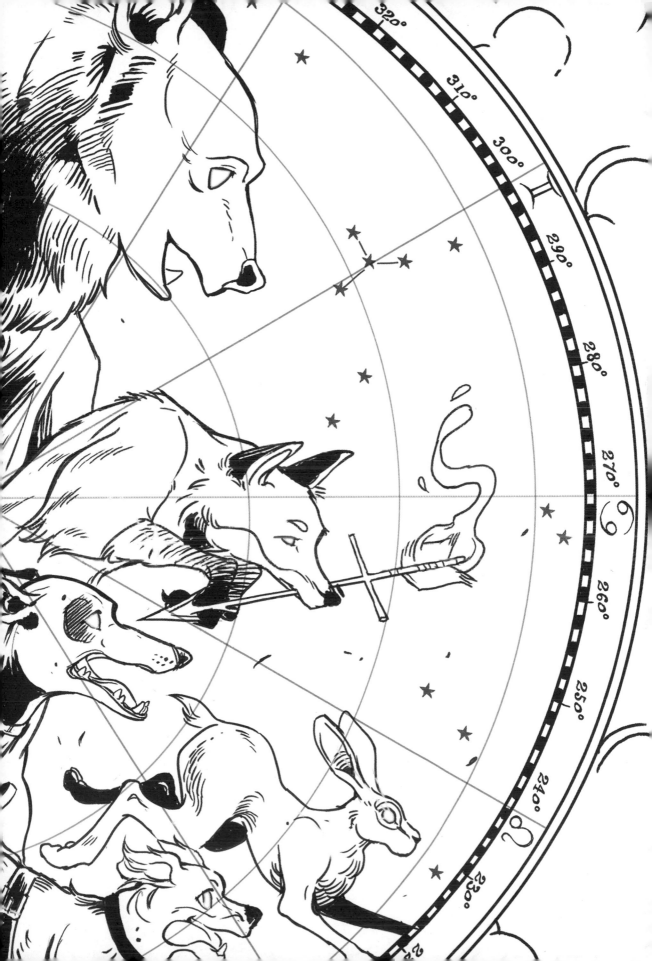

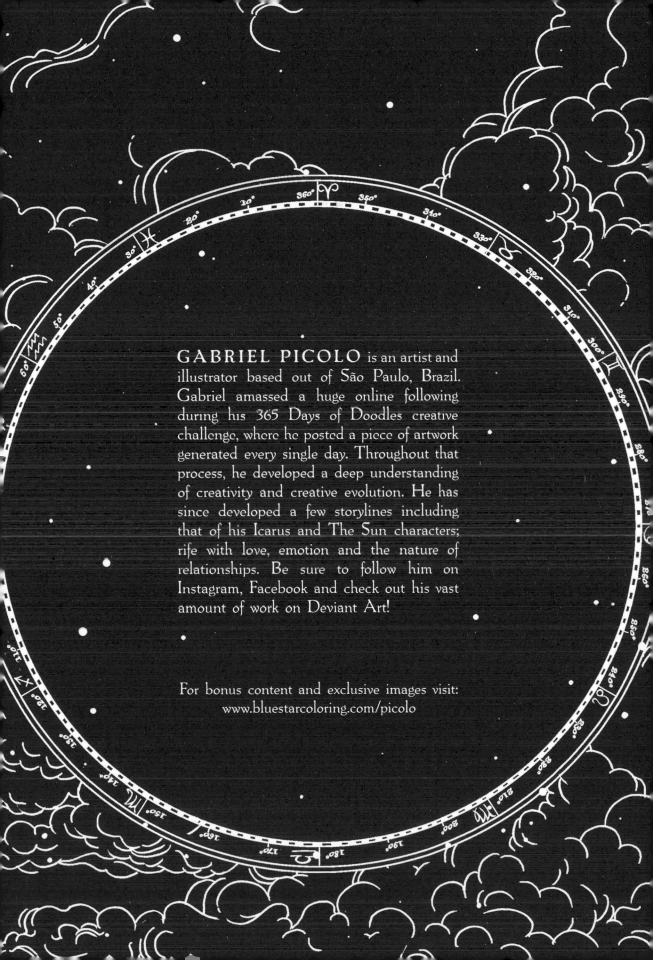

GABRIEL PICOLO is an artist and illustrator based out of São Paulo, Brazil. Gabriel amassed a huge online following during his 365 Days of Doodles creative challenge, where he posted a piece of artwork generated every single day. Throughout that process, he developed a deep understanding of creativity and creative evolution. He has since developed a few storylines including that of his Icarus and The Sun characters; rife with love, emotion and the nature of relationships. Be sure to follow him on Instagram, Facebook and check out his vast amount of work on Deviant Art!

For bonus content and exclusive images visit:
www.bluestarcoloring.com/picolo

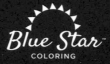

Blue Star
COLORING

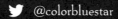

Blue Star Coloring launched in early 2015 with the release of *Stress Relieving Patterns*, our first adult coloring book to be featured on the New York Times Best Sellers list. Since then, we have released over 30 titles with the goal of promoting wellness and creativity worldwide. We feel fortunate to work with the independent artists we love, for the fans we love. Ultimately, our mission is to support the coloring community and help every person celebrate their own artist within!

www.bluestarcoloring.com

@bluestarcoloring   /bluestarcoloring

@colorbluestar